DOKOS, DHOTIS AND DAL

A Journey to the village of Gumlek in Nepal

by Anne Scott

To Paddey

Anne Scott

Forward and illustrations by Bill Scott

DOKOS, DHOTIS AND DAL

© Copyright Anne Scott 1997

Públished in Great Britain by

WF & AC Scott
North Cotes CE Primary School
North Cotes
GRIMSBY
NE Lincolnshire
DN36 5UZ

Illustrations and photographs by WF Scott.
First Impression September 1997.
Printed by:
EAST COAST GRAFIX, North Somercotes, Lincolnshire

ISBN 0-9531694-0-5

All profits from the sale of this book will go initially towards the building of the new school in Gumlek and subsequently to the Pahar Trust.

Front Cover: Young boy carrying water between the villages of Kahun and Gumlek.

Back Cover: Nepalese woman perched high up in a tree, chopping down branches for animal fodder.

This book is dedicated to
Tom, Chandra, Dhane
and
the villagers of Gumlek.

Bill and I with the Gumlek village committee and various visiting VIPs

ACKNOWLEDGEMENTS

My grateful thanks are due to Mr Fred Thompson for his help and encouragement and for proof reading the book; to Tom Langridge and Dhan Bahadur Chand for their help and advice; to Sally McBain for typing the text and to Jan Morris for preparing it for printing and to all the staff at North Cotes school for their valued support of this project.

CONTENTS

FORWARD

Meeting Tom was like winning the lottery. It was just before school camp in the June of 1995, I was sorting and tidying some NAHT Magazines. I had collected quite a pile of them, thinking that one day I would have the chance to skim through them, but there never is time. One heap, which was perched precariously on the arm of my lounge chair, slid to the floor and spilled open, 'Building Schools in the Mountains of Nepal' caught my eye, I picked it up and read on. It was an account of an ex-British Gurkha Officer named Tom Langridge and his close friend Chandra Bahadur Gurung building a school in Chandra Bahadur's village of Pokhari Tok. After reading the article I was so excited about the project and about their further exploits building schools in the mountains that I rang Tom that night. I asked if I too, and my school at North Cotes, could help fund and build a school in Nepal. So began a friendship link which began with Tom and his Gurkha friends stationed in England and grew, eventually linking with the hill village of Gumlek close to the Kali Gandaki River.

Tom soon visited the school and gave the children an excellent talk and slide show on Nepal and the building of the school at Pokhari Tok. He brought many gifts of Nepalese artifacts and seeing, touching and smelling these items began to give the children a real understanding and insight into the fascinating culture and way of life of the Nepalese. The children could smell the wood fire on the *chakati* - a sitting mat. They could feel the hand turned wood of the *theki* - yoghurt jug. They could see, touch and hear everything from a Nepalese umbrella - *shyakhu*, to the sound of a village drum - *madal*.

Our fund raising began in earnest and included, during our annual school camp of 1996 to the Lake District, sponsored summit bids on many Lakeland peaks including Skiddaw. This raised over £1500 and with the many other activities we had planned we were well on our way to raising the £8000 needed to build a school. By now Tom had given us news of a small hill village in Nepal called Gumlek which would make the perfect friendship link with North Cotes, it being of a similar size to ours and one in need of a new school. Gumlek was also the home village of Gurkha Dhan Bahadur Chand, presently stationed at Camberley Barracks in England. He was also a close friend of Tom and we were introduced to him when we visited Tom at his home. Dhane (for short!) and his friend Ghanga cooked us all a fine Nepalese curry and Anne and I felt at ease with them right from this, our first, meeting. They were just as my dad, who had served with a Gurkha regiment in the desert during the Second World War, had described the Gurkhas to me - short in size but incredibly fit and strong, with wide grins and impeccable manners. Dhane was also a keen Manchester United fan, which delighted me, being a Manchester lad.

Our work continued at school, and the children were building up a good knowledge of Nepal, its climate, topography and way of life. Soon letters from the pupils of Gumlek arrived for our children and pen friends were established for every child in the school. Our letters provided tremendous excitement for the children as they exchanged names, sports, pictures and photographs and wrote about each other's cultures, schools and home life. We soon realised the tremendous potential of our link with Gumlek. Our children were seeing, in a very real way, the poverty, beauty, resourcefulness, contentment, determination, endurance and creativity of the hill villagers of Nepal, by direct communication with their children. In contrast to our children's world of television, computer games, 'high tech' toys and electronic wizardry, theirs was one using their immediate environment to the full - be it collecting huge stacks of leafy branches as fodder for their animals, killing a bear with a wooden spear or swinging fearlessly round on a huge wooden fairground-type construction built at the edge of the village which makes The Big One in Blackpool look like a toy train!

There was so much material and first-hand experience coming from our link with Gumlek for us, as primary teachers, to use in the education of young children living in a rapidly progressing western world, about a Third World country. Soon there came a point in time when we just had to go out to Nepal and meet our friends in Gumlek. Such a visit would cement the relationship and I could bring back lots of photographs and first-hand knowledge of Gumlek for our children at North Cotes. I rang Tom one evening and we chatted about the possibility - which was the best season to go, flights, costs, vaccinations, language etc. I was determined to go and Tom was pleased to help me and set up his porters and his Pahar Trust people in Nepal to work out a schedule. The whole visit fell into place when news came that Dhane was about to take his leave and would be in Nepal for several months. He would be able to take us to his village of Gumlek himself. A date was fixed and flights were booked. Letters continued to be exchanged between the two schools and news also came via Gurkhas and Tom's friends in Kathmandu and Pokhara. The villagers of Gumlek had been working hard clearing and levelling a site for the new school and there were plans for us to dig and lay the foundation stone during our visit. I could hardly believe it, I have always loved mountains from being a small boy and later when I took up rock-climbing and mountaineering, Nepal, the Himalaya and Everest were constant subjects of my reading. I never dreamt that I would actually be visiting and seeing the places I had read so much about in mountaineering expedition books. However, to me there is also something else quite fantastic about this link. I have been a teacher for 25 years and am, by nature, a practical person. Teaching has given me a great deal of joy and satisfaction but as a primary teacher you never quite see the end product - unlike being a welder or some such occupation where you can say to your own children as you ride by in your car. "Your dad helped to build that bridge or that skyscraper up there." The nearest you come, is when you are stopped in the shopping precinct one Saturday afternoon by a tall twenty-five year old saying "Hello Mr. Scott!" You look at the young man and struggle to recognise him as your brain sorts through the hundreds of children you have had in your class. You stop for a chat, "How are you getting on?" "What are you doing?" You finally walk away with the pleasant feeling that you helped him to get there. This friendship link is going to fulfil a life-time ambition of wanting to build something concrete - a school at Gumlek in Nepal. It will also bring so many benefits to my own pupils at North Cotes and will create so much opportunity for the education of young children in Nepal.

The work from our link with Gumlek continues and can be seen in the letters, books and displays of our children at North Cotes and in the ethos and tone of our small rural school. It can also be seen in the little hill village of Gumlek in the faces of the children and villagers and in the school that is rising out of the clearing. The labour is provided by the villagers, the know-how and civil engineering by the trained Gurkha soldiers who live in Gumlek and the funds to buy the materials are raised by the pupils of North Cotes. The whole team has been trained and put together by the Pahar Trust, spearheaded by two exceptional Gurkhas, Tom Langridge and Chandra Bahadur Gurung.

Our visit to Nepal was the most memorable and exciting journey of my life so far and our welcome in Gumlek truly amazing. There is not a day goes by when we don't feed off the memories of that journey and think of Nepal and the new friends that we have made. The following is an account of that journey through Nepal written by my wife and trekking partner, Anne.

Bill Scott.

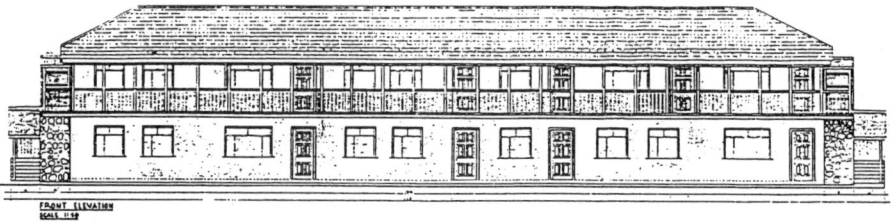

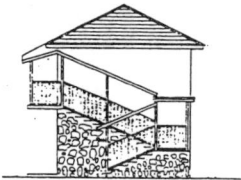

Plans of the school to be built in Gumlek.

INTRODUCTION

When we took on the Friendship Link with Shree Sahabir school in Gumlek, Nepal, we were given the opportunity to visit a part of Nepal seldom, if ever, visited by any Europeans. Consequently, this account of my first visit seen through a woman's eyes provides a unique insight into the way of life in a true Nepalese village, a life which has changed very little over hundreds of years and hopefully which will change very little over the next few hundred years. My experiences in parts II and III will be more familiar to seasoned trekkers in Nepal and I make no apologies for my naive approach as a first-time visitor - my account will be of interest to anyone who loves to travel. On returning to England I bought the November issue of TGO magazine and was poignantly reminded of my visit when I read Mike Harding's column about his trek to Mera Peak. He writes: "People come from the West expecting it to be quaint and clean, like the travel brochures. When they find that it's exactly the opposite, they can't handle it. They can't see through all the dirt and the smells and disease to the beauty that lies beyond."

Nepal is dramatic, fascinating and a tremendously beautiful and friendly country, and I have had the privilege to enjoy three very contrasting areas in as many weeks. Do not visit Nepal with any pre-conceived ideas and you will fall in love with the country 'warts and all', which is exactly what I did.

PART I - GUMLEK

Chapter 1 - CULTURE SHOCK

"I carry bags!"

"I carry!"

"You give me English pound coin!"

"One English pound coin!"

This from all quarters, as, in an exhausted and bewildered state, our flight having been delayed some six hours in Dubai, my husband, Bill, and I peered through the darkness, trying to catch a glimpse of our Gurkha friend Dhane who was to meet us at the airport. Thankfully, Dhane's face appeared through the gloom, only just recognisable from a previous meeting in England some six months before. Bags were grabbed from us - much to my relief as, in our enthusiasm to bring as many gifts for the children of Gumlek as possible, our baggage weight was well over the airline allowance.

"Let me handle this" said Dhane authoritatively as more demands for English pound coins were heard and tussles had broken out amongst the boys over the right to carry our bags. The going rate, we were to learn later, was about ten rupees each so the lad who, in the initial confusion, managed to relieve us of a pound coin, equivalent to eighty-five rupees at the current exchange rate, had made a killing which probably kept him in cigarettes for the next six months! One pound for carrying two heavy bags some two hundred yards to a waiting taxi is a fair price by British standards but this was our first example of how over-generosity by tourists can cause problems of inflation and greed eventually leading to crime amongst the Nepalese, who see tourists as having far too much money that they do not value. Who can blame them for taking advantage?

Although it was about 9.30 pm and dark, the air was warm and humid as we piled into the ancient taxi which rattled along following the rear light of Dhane's motorbike ahead. Most forms of transport in Nepal are ancient, unreliable and uncomfortable. The springing has to withstand the lumps and bumps of the average Nepalese roads - few of which are more than a hardened mud track with the odd stretch of tarmac. These stretches of 'proper' road are often more hazardous than the stony mud tracks (where at least it is impossible to drive more than fifteen to twenty miles per hour) as drivers tend to take full advantage of the (slightly!) smoother road surface and drive at breakneck speed with total disregard for any bends - which are mostly hairpin without any sort of barrier to prevent vehicles plummeting off the edge.

This short taxi trip was relatively calm compared to the journeys in various Nepalese modes of transport that were to follow, the driver merely honking his horn at thirty second intervals while twisting and turning to avoid potholes, other traffic and a huge dead buffalo lying in the middle of the road, which nobody seemed to be making any attempt to remove.

A car is an extremely valuable commodity in Nepal, especially a European car which is of superior quality to the majority which are Indian. This is particularly true in Kathmandu and the other big towns where a car is so vital for transporting the weak and helpless tourists, unable to carry loads of more than a few kilos, from airport to hotel to tourist spots. Consequently they must be made to last as long as possible and the roads are littered with cars, trucks and buses in various states of repair often with groups of five or six Nepalis squatting underneath discussing the state of play. Hold-ups due to mechanical faults are frequent on the buses and passengers wait patiently, sometimes for hours, for on-the-spot repairs, offering help or advice according to their capabilities. There are few regulations when it comes to transport, with hardly any road rules, no control over the safety of vehicles or their emissions and no driving test to speak of so that you risk your life merely crossing a road. In Kathmandu, the sudden increase in traffic over the past few years has led to serious air pollution with filthy black car emissions mixed with the dust from the roads causing a visible layer of 'smog' over the town in the dry season and necessitating the wearing of masks by regular commuters.

Dhane's house, being on the outskirts of Kathmandu, provided a relatively peaceful haven away from the busy centre. Our initial meeting and contact with Dhane's family was brief as we were late arriving and had an early flight to Pokhara the next morning. Sunita, Dhane's wife, had cooked us a typical Nepalese meal of very mildly curried pork with rice, *dal* and a green

1 Staff and pupils on the summit of Skiddaw during our sponsored climbs in the Lake District in the summer of 1996.

2 Above: The weigh-in. Keeping the baggage weight-allowance proved difficult, Sarah steps on the scales with the holdall of gifts. 3 Below: Final assembly with the children handing in their gifts and letters for us to take to Gumlek.

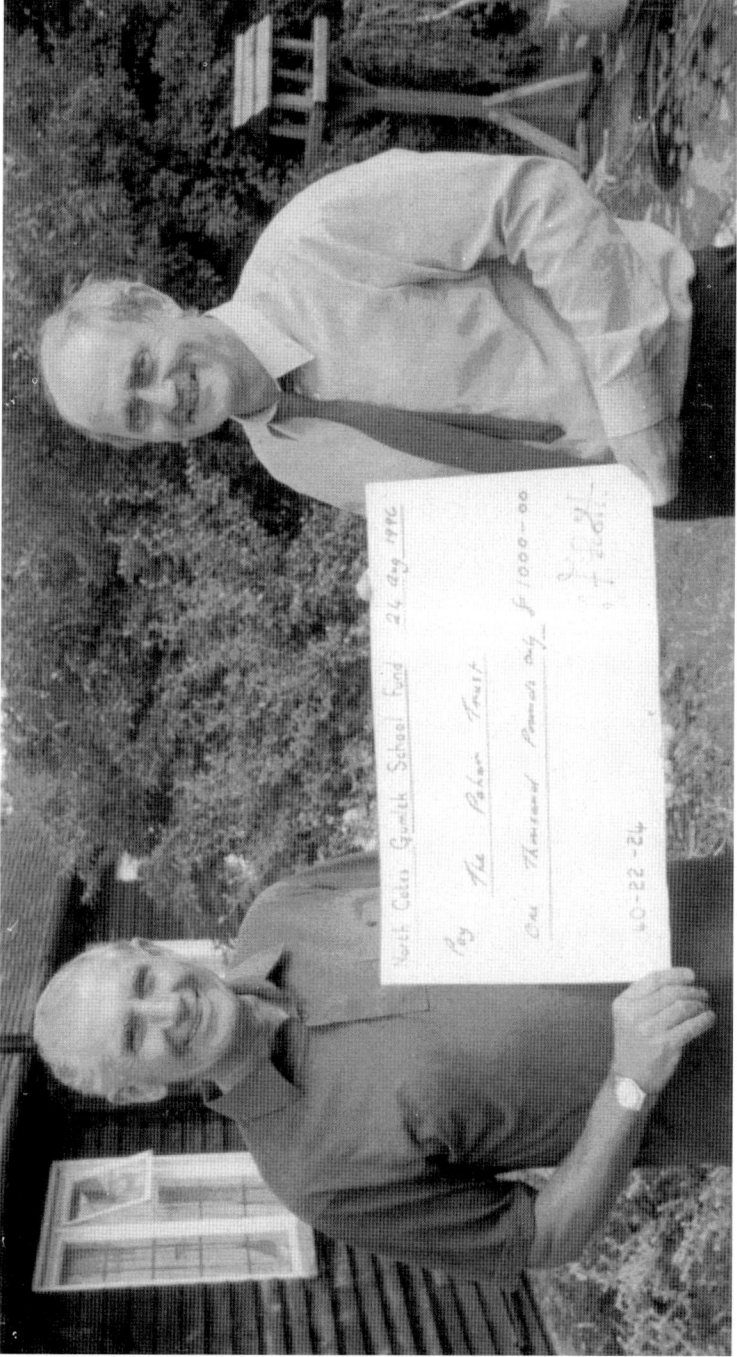

4 Bill (right) presenting Tom with a cheque towards the Gumlek fund.

5 Dhane's children Smriti and Sandeep getting a lift to school.

6 Dhane, his wife Sunita and two children Smriti and Sandeep.

7 Gam and his wife and two daughters outside their hotel.

8 Dhane, Chandra and Bill relaxing on the verandah at Twin Peaks.

9 Buffaloes, cows, goats, pigs and wild dogs roam the streets of Pokhara.

10 Small shops in Pokhara selling just about everything you need.

11 The Annapurna range from the roof of Twin Peaks Hotel.

12 Shopkeepers in Damauli.

13 Crossing the suspension bridge from Damauli at the start of our trek to Gumlek.

vegetable resembling spinach. Smriti, their eight year old daughter, had stayed up to see us and we were to become totally enchanted by both her and her younger brother, Sandeep, as we got to know them better at the end of our stay.

It was with some relief that I crawled into bed only to be rudely awakened after an hour or so by the loud and strident yapping of a dog. The barking continued all night, on and off, being passed from one dog to another, some in the immediate vicinity, some further away, so the baying was relentless. This is something Sunita and the children get used to but even Dhane finds it disturbing when returning for six months leave after living in the U.K. for three years. Subsequent nights in Kathmandu were spent with wax earplugs firmly in place but I was afraid I would not hear the alarm clock carefully set for 6.00 am, so I spent a fitful first night waiting for the sounds of morning. These came sooner than expected at about 4.30 am even before the first light. Then came the famous Nepalese 'cough' consisting of noisy clearing of the throat followed by spitting. This was swiftly followed by a male voice greeting the morning with doleful singing to the accompaniment of pans clattering and bells ringing as people began their day with prayers to the gods. Of necessity the Nepalese day starts early, making full use of the daylight hours which last until about 6.30 pm. Most Nepalese are in bed by 8.30 - 9.00 pm as they do not have electric light. There is a basic electricity supply in Kathmandu but only the better off houses and shops are supplied. The villages rely on hydro-electric or solar power, kerosene lamps and candles.

Abandoning all attempts to sleep I went out onto the verandah and up some spiral stairs to the flat roof of the house. The rest of Kathmandu could be seen to the north while to the west I looked down on the winding Bagmati river which runs across the south of the city. Several houses built on the banks of this river had slowly slipped into it and one or two more looked decidedly shaky and 'out of true'. There is subsidence in this area and in the past there have been a few earthquakes. Consequently the emphasis, when building a house in Nepal, is on strength. After the foundations, which are probably deeper than ours, and the thick concrete floor, the walls are built about nine inches thick and solid. The ceiling and first floor is then made by supporting corrugated iron and wooden shuttering to form a thick box shape on rows and rows of wooden stakes. Concrete is then poured into the 'box' and the stakes and corrugated iron removed when it is set. The resulting 'corrugated ceiling' is a feature of many house interiors where the concrete has merely been painted white underneath. Houses are often built in stages with subsequent storeys built above the ground floor in the same way. Windows do not always have glass but have instead an iron grid, for security, with fine wire mesh behind to keep out the mosquitoes and then wooden shutters. This method of construction does not provide any insulation and houses in Kathmandu can be cold in winter when night temperatures can fall to below freezing. Insulating materials such as wallpaper and carpeting are expensive as they have to be brought in from other countries and the cost of electricity is high for the average family. In contrast to the town houses the village homesteads can be much warmer with their fires and the natural insulating properties of the mud and wood construction.

Although I had read many books on Nepal, including the ubiquitous 'Lonely Planet' guide from cover to cover, nothing had prepared me for my first glimpse of Kathmandu in the daylight. Even from the relatively secure confines of the inside of the taxi which took us to the internal Kathmandu airport, I was shocked by the dirt and pollution, only a little of which had been experienced the previous evening. Now, in the daylight, I could see the heaps of rubbish piled at the side of the road, some reduced to a sodden mass by the recent rain. I was not fully prepared for the sight of families living only feet from the busy road, at best in corrugated iron and polythene shacks and at worst under sheets of polythene or blue plastic sheeting draped between the trees. Even the shops were little more than concrete or wooden sheds with a small room at the back where the whole family lived. Poverty screamed at me from every angle and it seemed that everyone was out on the street trying to sell something. The road itself was a seething mass of cars, trucks, buses, bicycles and motorbikes all weaving their way in and out of each other to the sound of tremendous honking and hooting of horns. Every motorbike had at least one pillion passenger and sometimes two or three children would be sat astride the petrol tank and on the handlebars while wives would be precariously perched side-saddle on the back with saris flying in the breeze. None of the passengers were wearing helmets as in Nepal only the driver is compelled to wear a helmet. Later on we were to experience Kathmandu on foot but by then we were more prepared. For the present, I closed the window to shut out the dust and tried to come to terms with this, my first experience of a Third World country.

What happened to all the families in the winter when the night time temperature drops to below freezing? How did the scantily clad children keep warm? Would the roadside sellers make enough money to keep their families once all the tourists had gone home? Some of them were there doing seasonal work digging drains, perhaps they moved on when the work ran out. My immediate reaction was to rush out and give them the money they so desperately needed, bundle the children up and take them away to a better life. But of course this was impossible and I was left with a feeling of helplessness.

On arrival at the airport we were once again mobbed by boys anxious to carry our bags and this time the going rate of ten rupees each was duly paid. Our bags were carefully weighed by an ancient manual weighing machine and we were eyed suspiciously while two of them were opened. This seemed to be more of a formality than a proper search as the zips were smoothly closed again after a peremptory glance in each. The checking of hand luggage involved Bill and Dhane going one way and me another to a small cubicle behind a faded curtain where sat a kindly looking Nepalese lady who merely asked me to open the zip of the lid of my daysac. Upon finding nothing more exciting than some rolled up loo paper in a polythene bag she smiled and waved me on. I could have had the Nepalese crown jewels for all she knew! We waited in a large bare room with the now familiar concrete walls and floor for the internal flight that would take us to Pokhara. Chairs were arranged in rows back-to-back and facing each other and in the corner was a kiosk selling newspapers and bottled drinks. This internal airport was very much a poor relation of the main international airport we had arrived at. A lad who looked about twelve but was probably older was mopping the floor with huge side-to-side swings of a damp and filthy mop. With the patience that only the Nepalese possess, he would be doing this all day long for a few rupees. Not knowing when I would get the next opportunity I decided to try the airport loos. These were the typical Asian toilets with two foot rests and a hole to squat over. They were quite passable compared to some I encountered later so long as I held my nose and lifted my skirt well clear of the floor!

Chapter 2 - POKHARA

The flight to Pokhara was fascinating. This was our first glimpse of Nepal from the air and we were low enough to see the typical terraced hills and fields of rice, maize and millet. We followed the winding Madi and Seti rivers and I was able to pick out one of the Pahar Trust schools that had already been built in this area, perched on top of a hill, looking splendid in the green landscape. During the flight we were presented with a sweet to suck during take-off and a cardboard box with two pastries inside to eat! Such luxury I didn't expect but we were to meet many examples of the Nepalese striving to meet European standards in an effort to encourage tourism which is their only industry. As we travelled through the country we became more and more aware of the two standards that exist side-by-side - tourist standard and Nepalese standard with a corresponding tourist price and Nepali price. This applied not only to hotels and restaurants but also to food in shops, bus fares and admission to tourist attractions.

Pokhara airport is little more than a large muddy field and Pokhara, the wettest place in Nepal, had still not quite finished its monsoon. We paddled across to the corrugated iron roofed shack which served as a reception area where Chandra, the Pahar Trust co-ordinator in Nepal, was there to meet us. His full name is Chandra Bahadur Gurung and he too is an ex-Gurkha who has served in the British army. Once again our taxi was led to the hotel by Chandra on his motorbike. Twin Peaks hotel is a mid-price hotel by Nepalese standards in the Fewa Lakeside area a little away from the town. The sign outside proudly announces "We are invironmentally friendly" (this spelling was pretty good compared to other signs and notices we saw!) and "Proprietor - Gam Gurung, ex-British Gurkha soldier." The hotel presented an impressive façade with balconies and arches and an 'English-style garden' with flower-beds, pergolas and even outside electric lighting. In the reception area was a whole list of features guaranteed to impress the tourist such as:- Full continental and English menu, spectacular rooftop view, hot and cold showers, laundry service, filtered water, room service, attached bathroom -even Sky TV! The view from the rooftop really is spectacular - on a clear day you can see the whole of the Annapurna range, dominated by the Fishtail towering above you, but you have to get up at 5.30 am before the cloud covers the mountains.

However, the best thing about Twin Peaks is Gam himself - you really do 'come as a guest and leave as a friend' as it says on the door, and in our case we felt friends straight away, such was the welcome we received. Gam's English is immaculate and he is an avid follower of British football, having spent some sixteen years in England whilst serving as a British Gurkha. Our room was large, with its own balcony overlooking the garden and the attached bathroom had bath, shower, washbasin and English toilet.This was indeed luxury to us, being used to camping in both the UK and on the continent. The price of a double room per night was about £18 - £26, and all meals were extra. You'd be hard pressed to find a B&B in England for this and since nearly all the main courses were less than one hundred rupees (about £1.20) the food was very cheap too. We, as members of the Pahar Trust, also received quite a big discount off the cost of the room.

Encouraged by Gam, we set off to sample the local tourist spot which was the famous Lake Fewa itself. Here again there is a magnificent view of the Annapurna range and the Fishtail but again a clear day is needed.

An umbrella is a very useful piece of equipment in Nepal, both against the rain and the sun. Today was a scorcher and I sat in a long canoe under my umbrella feeling a bit like the African Queen as Dhane paddled us across the lake. In the middle there is an island where stands a Hindu temple, closely guarded by an elderly Nepalese woman who makes sure that nobody who isn't Hindu crosses the threshold. All around the temple were the usual traders trying to sell us posters, postcards, jewellery and the like.

Back on land, away from the relative peace of the lake, Pokhara is a very busy place. The streets - one could stretch a point and call them avenues - are wider than in Kathmandu and lined from end to end with shops selling goods of every description. The saying 'in Kathmandu you can buy anything' seems to apply equally to Pokhara. I had been fretting, ever since my watch battery ran out on the plane, about managing for three weeks without a watch but only a hundred yards or so from the hotel was a shop which fitted a new battery, cleaned the watch and synchronized the date in a few minutes - all for 120 rupees. As Pokhara is one of the main starting points for trekkers, shops offering to buy, sell, exchange or hire secondhand gear of every description featured prominently. In fact you could come here wearing the clothes you stand up in and kit yourself out fully, so long as you're not fussy about the odd bed bug in your sleeping bag and don't look too carefully at some rather suspicious looking stains inside! Trekkers who travel with unreliable airlines frequently have to do just this when their luggage ends up in Delhi or Sydney or other distant parts of the world.

Nearing the centre of the town the shops changed from the corrugated iron stall-type construction to something fractionally more substantial with cement covered brick or stone walls. Brilliantly coloured cotton materials hung from shop fronts and hanks of wool dyed in the brightest hues imaginable spilled out onto the road. You can even buy loose powder dyes which are gaudily displayed in huge boxes. I saw really good quality furniture being made, blacksmiths, welders, tailors busy on ancient treadle sewing machines, colourful plastic buckets and water containers in huge toppling stacks, barrows piled high with fruit and vegetables of every description interspersed with grocery shops where packets of coffee, nuts and crisps tended to be either hung up on strings like gaily coloured flags or suspended in what looked like a fisherman's landing net. Every so often would be a shop advertising Fax machines, Satellite TV or "Computers Sold Here". Of course there were the usual tourist shops selling Tibetan crafts, jewellery, books, maps, beautiful sandalwood carvings, carpets and T-shirts especially embroidered while you wait with anything you like - these were mostly of the wear-once-and-throw-away variety as neither the colours nor the fabric looked as though they would stand up to the rigours of a western washing machine. Negotiating the streets was quite a risky business as you have to be ready to leap out of the way of a honking car, truck or bicycle complete with crossbar passenger, which comes whizzing towards you out of nowhere, its rider shouting "Hello" cheekily. Moving at a slower pace but no less hazardous are the wandering cows and buffalo. These animals have the complete run of the town and amble about nonchalantly, nibbling indiscriminately at everything from flowers in hotel gardens, vegetables on the many stalls to old cardboard boxes, a huge one of which I saw being systematically devoured by a quite healthy - looking beast as if it were the best thing since sliced bread. It must do wonders for the flavour of the milk! They tend to plonk themselves down in the middle of the road, carelessly swishing their tails, safe in the knowledge that the whole of the town's traffic could come to a standstill before anyone attempted to move them. Some of the buffalo, particularly, can give you quite a nasty swipe with their horns if you happen to catch them in a bad mood - I happened to be wearing a bright red T-shirt that day so I gave them a fairly wide berth. Families of ducks and chickens and even pigs and the odd goat scuttled about ready to trip you up should you take your eyes off where you are putting your feet. Here, in the centre of the town, we must have stuck out like sore thumbs with our pale skins, cameras and trainers - the Nepalese all wear flip-flops - and we were pestered by street traders suddenly producing gifts and tourist trinkets for us to buy, but more distressingly by young children or older men and women often with a child in tow begging for money and food. Some of them had parts of legs or arms missing or were deaf, blind or physically handicapped in other ways and all were painfully thin. This problem is not as bad in Pokhara as it is in Kathmandu but all tourists are asked not to encourage begging so we had to walk on.

It was by now mid-afternoon and, feeling a bit peckish, we chose what looked to be a pleasant little cafe with tables outside - if a little grubby round the edges. Dhane assured us that this was 'tourist standard' so we sat down. Bottled drinks such as coke and 7-Up were on sale at only fifteen rupees which was cheaper than the bottled water which could be as much as twenty-five rupees. Our thirst quenched, we decided on a plate of chips each and then something called Tibetan bread to follow. The chips were delicious, if you ignored the black bits and the Tibetan bread turned out to be a flattish dough-based affair about the size and texture of a small pizza base which had been deep-fried so that it puffed up into a crispy golden pancake and then drizzled with honey. Two half cherries provided the finishing touches and from then on we were sold on the stuff and every eating place was judged by the quality of its Tibetan bread.

The rest of the afternoon was spent at the Tibetan village in Pokhara which is a village of refugees originally from Tibet who settled there and now make their living by selling their extensive range of craft and jewellery to the tourists. Knowing a little of the history and plight of the Tibetans, and having had strict instructions from my daughter to bring back a Tibetan 'singing bowl' I decided it was worth supporting their cause. The man at the booking office for the famous Pokhara to Kathmandu bus later informed us that in his opinion the Tibetan villagers were better off than the Nepalese but he also tried to persuade us to stay at his guest house rather than Twin Peaks as it was only four dollars a night (about £3).

The Tibetan village has its own school and rows of little houses. The stalls are all run by very persuasive ladies who beckoned us with encouragements such as "Come and look" "Only looking, free." "You buy, I give you good price." As soon as we ventured within an imaginary demarcation line about one metre from the stall, they rushed out with stools for us to sit on so that they could show us their wares. As this was only the start of our trip our intentions were to 'just look' and return later to do our shopping. We managed to get away with buying a couple of bone bracelets and two necklaces so long as we promised to come back at the end of our stay. We did, in fact, go back when we returned from Gumlek and made several pounds worth of purchases. Our faces had not been forgotten and we were careful to buy from two of the three stalls we had visited. Nearly spent up, we thought we could sneak past the third one but the stallholder wasn't having any of it and rushed out after us calling "You promise, you promise, you come back!" followed by an angry stream of Nepali. She pressed into my hand what was in actual fact quite a nice bangle with a delicate filigree design and entreated Bill to buy a Tibetan calender stamped on a large square pendant. The five hundred rupees we parted with for both I felt was well worth it as I wasn't quite sure what retribution might have befallen us had we tried to escape!

We headed back to Twin Peaks for a welcome shower - we were in luck as the sun had been beating down all day and hot water was available from the solar heating panels on the roof. We had not yet tired of the Nepalese food which Gam seemed eager to offer and we ordered well in advance, which is necessary at all eating places in Nepal to allow the kitchen staff time to cook the meal. The food arrived on a small stainless steel tray which was divided into six sections. The middle one in front was for meat which in this case was chicken with a mild curry flavour, although this was not nice neat cubes of chicken as you would eat in England but bones with little bits of meat attached. Gam assured us that this is the way the Nepalese like it: "English meat has no flavour, all flavour near the bones." In fact most Nepalese crunch the bones, skin and the lot. I wondered what happened to the breast meat which we never saw but came to the conclusion that Nepalese chickens are not the plump, factory-fed, flavourless birds, that we are accustomed to but are much thinner creatures with less breast meat but more flavour. To the left of the tray were potatoes in a spicy sauce. Carrying on round in a clockwise direction, next was a hottish chutney, then a huge mound of boiled rice and then another dish of beans and root vegetables also in a fairly mildly spiced sauce. The *dal* or lentil soup, green in colour, was served separately in a small bowl and this you tipped on the rice. Traditionally the Nepalese eat with the fingers of their right hand, scooping the food together in quite an expert way. They also seem to have huge appetites and the waiters kept bringing out more of everything so you can eat as much as you want. A Nepalese breakfast is quite small, especially in the villages where it may be only a handful of popcorn eaten on the way to the fields. Lunchtime is fairly early - eleven-ish - when people eat a huge cooked meal of rice and *dal* but this has to last them until late evening when, after all the work is done, they eat another huge meal again of rice, *dal*, sometimes vegetables and occasionally meat.

The next day was the start of our trek to Gumlek and we had been instructed by Chandra to have our bags ready by 7.00 am when the porters would come and collect them. Determined to get a good night's sleep, I wedged my earplugs in, against the sound of the ever barking dogs, having been assured by Dhane that he would bang loudly on the door at 6.00 am to make sure we were up.

Chapter 3 - A WET START

The day dawned cloudy and dull so there was still no rooftop view. However we were down in reception, bags duly packed ready to go, at 7.00 am. A few minutes later a telephone call came from Chandra to say that the porters hadn't arrived yet so we were to put everything on hold and meet at the bus stop near his house at 8.00 am. The porters were obviously going by 'Nepali time' which gives a pretty wide margin either way of an hour or so. We dawdled over breakfast as a steady drizzle started to fall. By the time we got to the bus stop, Pokhara was living up to its reputation of being the wettest place in Nepal and the clouds were absolutely chucking it down. I still had my trusty umbrella and Dhane skipped across the road which was now nearly a river, returning with two more umbrellas which proved to be very temperamental throughout the rest of the trip, just about managing to stay in one piece for the three weeks that they were needed!

There were two types of bus going to Damauli as there are to most tourist areas - the local bus and the tourist bus. The local bus is a 'stopper' taking twice as long for the journey because it stops at every little village and the tourist bus is faster, slightly more comfortable inside and, of course, more expensive. We plumped for the local bus which happened to come along first, duly paid the tourist fare for ourselves and the Nepali fare for Dhane and the four porters and were ushered to the 'best' seats in the front of the bus behind the driver where there was slightly more leg room. Our bags safely (we hoped!) strapped onto the roof, we trundled off, but not before the driver had pressed his horn for a full two minutes; two runners had scouted the immediate vicinity, whistling loudly, in the hope of gaining more passengers and finally leapt nimbly aboard, banging the side of the bus as they did so as a signal to the driver that he could go. Not satisfied with this he drove up and down the full length of the main street of Pokhara three times to the accompaniment of more honking and whistling just to make quite sure he had collected all possible passengers.

The bus itself was a very jolly affair, all the buses are privately owned and the cab and rear windows especially are gaily decorated with sparkling tinsel, frilly lace trimming and brightly coloured tassels to make the journey more colourful! The slogans on the back such as 'Drive slow, be safe' and 'Get there safely,' are absolutely meaningless as it is every driver's aim to 'get there' as fast as possible, cramming on as many passengers as he can. Ours seemed to have a problem with his handbrake as every time we stopped, he put the bus in gear. I just hoped there weren't too many hills!

The road out of Pokhara ran between green rice and millet fields with the polythene and corrugated iron shacks near the road in sharp contrast to the well-built attractive houses further back. Everything looked very green as we left the town behind and all along the roadside children were walking to school or waiting for the school bus. There are two types of schools in Nepal, the government schools and the private schools. The former are free, for those who wish to attend, up to the age of nine years and the latter have to be paid for. There is a world of difference between these two systems, the private school children look very smart, if a little worn and mud splattered, in their uniforms - pleated skirts or pinafore dresses for the girls with contrasting blouses, socks and even hair ribbons, and shirts and ties for the boys. Although there seemed to be a preference for sky blue and navy the colours of the uniforms were various - green and yellow, red and white, (rather impractical in the rainy season!) burgundy and blue, blue and white. In some schools the teachers also have a uniform. Footwear in the private schools is proper shoes and socks while the government school children wear flip-flops if they have any shoes at all. There is a uniform of sorts but not all children can afford it. Attendance too is erratic, particularly in the villages where the family wor-kload is so great that some children need to stay at home to work in the fields or may only attend school part-time. English is taught as a second language in both types of school but the standard of teaching is much better in the private schools and children are made to work harder. In fact if you ever get lost, ask a teenager in school uniform for directions, he is a perfect gentleman, his English will be excellent and he will be pleased and honoured both to help you and to show off his command of the English language.

The bus stopped and started its way along the bumpy road to Damauli, picking up more and more passengers until I was sure we couldn't cram any more on but every time it stopped somebody managed to move along another

The "Pahar Trust Kit" included everything except the kitchen sink!

couple of inches and make room for one more. We had been warned that Damauli would be very hot but today, when we finally arrived some three hours later, we stepped out into torrential rain and had to seek the shelter of a nearby 'hotel'. This one was definitely not tourist standard but the owners offered us seats and drinks of coke while the porters ate a huge meal to fortify them for the task ahead. Each of them was carrying some sixty kilos packed into the conical shaped baskets called *dokos* which were carried on their backs with the full weight being taken by a band round their heads. This is the way the Nepalese carry everything from water pots to school bags and even crates of chickens. In fact Dhane told us that for a while after he came to England as a Gurkha soldier, his head was quite flat at the front from carrying heavy loads in this way. I couldn't imagine what was in the four *dokos* as our three holdalls all fitted into just one of them. We later discovered that the Pahar Trust Kit comprised a full canteen of stainless steel cups, plates, bowls, teapots, jugs and cutlery, several huge saucepans, pressure cookers, kerosene stoves and lamps, mattresses, tents and ground sheets, together with such refinements as toothpicks, paper napkins, a wooden toilet seat and six loo rolls!

While we were waiting I surveyed the scene. Outside were dozens of stalls selling bananas, apples, various vegetables including a long parsnip shaped one that was a type of radish, and a cross between a cucumber and a marrow. Heaps of dried maize and other dried pulses overflowed from barrows and stalls. The stallholders waited patiently with their goods, either sitting on the barrows sheltering from the rain or standing under umbrellas at the side. The usual buffaloes were wandering about and people nipped backwards and forwards tying on a sheet of polythene here and adjusting a tarpaulin there. I carried on a sign language conversation with an older woman in the cafe who was anxious to know whether Bill and I were married, how many and how old our children were, and of course where we had come from and where we were going. She had a huge growth on her neck which surely would have been dealt with at a much earlier stage in the western world but which didn't seem to be bothering her too much.

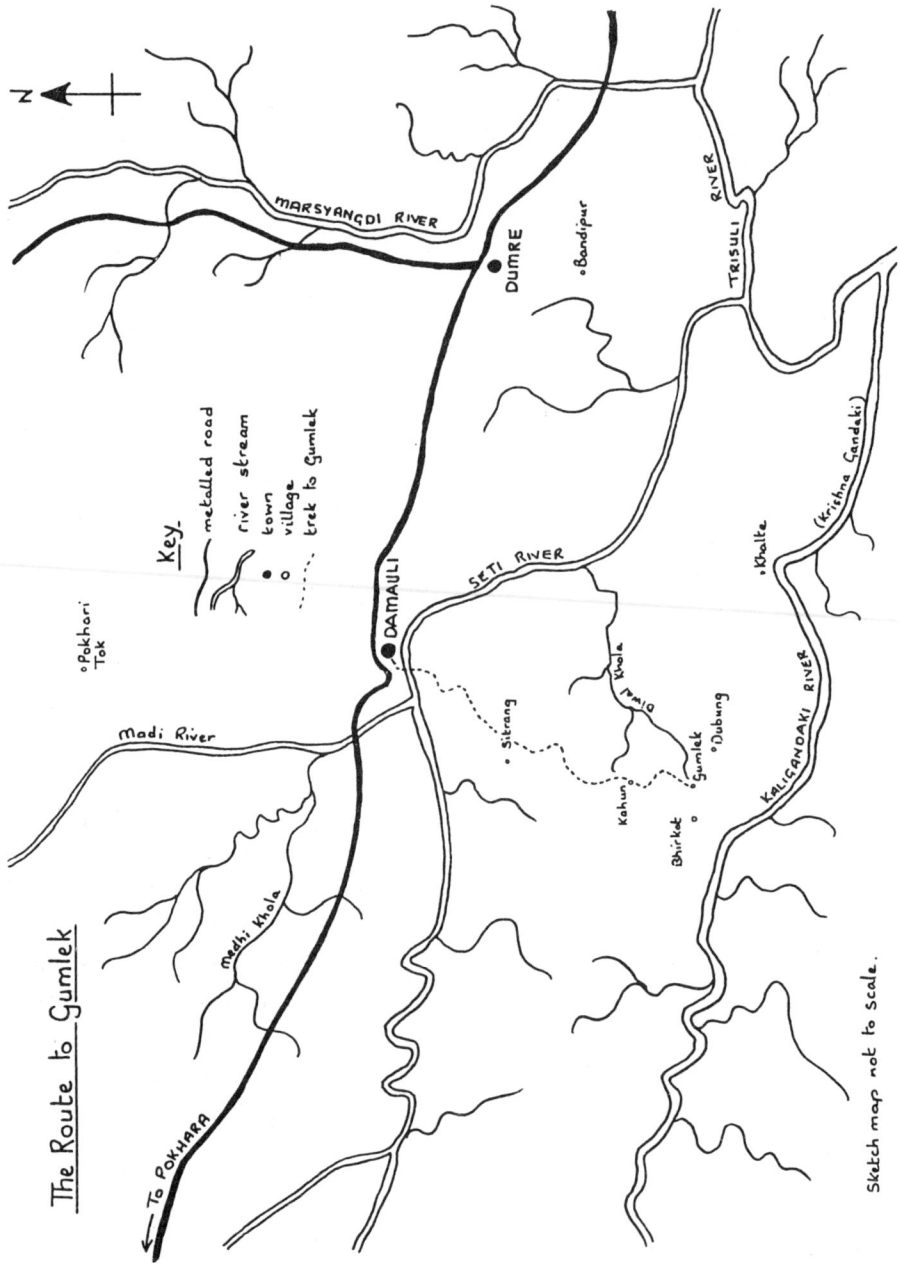

The Route to Gumlek

Key.
metalled road
river stream
town
village
trek to Gumlek

N

MARSYANGDI RIVER

DUMRE
●Bandipur

TRISULI RIVER

(Krishna Gandaki)

SETI RIVER

DAMAULI

oPokhari
Tok

Madi River

●Sitrang

Kahun Khola

Madi Khola

oPokhari
Tok

Bhirkot
o

Gumlek
o

oDubung

●Khalte

KALIGANDAKI RIVER

To POKHARA ←

Sketch map not to scale.

30

Chapter 4 - *NAMASTES* AND JUNGLE DRUMS

We finally set off for Gumlek at about 11.30, umbrellas held aloft against the rain which had eased off only slightly. My skirt, totally impractical in the circumstances, was flapping soddenly round my calves. I had been advised to wear a longish skirt rather than trousers in this remote area where women rarely show anything above the ankle, and where villagers might be offended by shorts or trousers. Dhane, like Rabbit in 'Winnie the Pooh', has many friends-and-relations and as we walked through the town he made a swift diversion to call on one of them. While we waited, a pair of girls came out from a nearby school, pristine in their white dresses, and eyed us curiously as they waited to use the loo. A cheery wave from me sent them into giggles and they scuttled back to the classroom to report on the strange creatures they had seen.

Dhane returned, his friend-and-relation not at home and we set off again, first crossing the Seti River by means of a long metal suspension bridge. For anyone who gets nervous walking along wooden piers or has any sort of vertigo this could have been a problem but fortunately I have never suffered from such fears and I strode out confidently. Pride comes before a fall, however, and I managed to get my stick (a vital piece of equipment handed to me by Chandra before we set off) stuck between the metal strips of the bridge and ruined the whole performance with an ungainly stagger to the side setting the whole bridge swinging and causing great amusement to a group of children approaching in the opposite direction!

There followed a steep climb through jungle for some three hours and it was here that we realised that our Gortex waterproofs brought from home were quite unsuitable, being far too hot for these humid conditions, and that we were better off in T-shirts and umbrellas, although Bill's seemed to spend its time either soggily draped over his face or inside out catching the rain and periodically emptying its contents every time it caught in a branch!

Eager to practise our *Namaste* we greeted everyone we met on the track. Dhane, being the local boy who had made it into the Gurkhas, was known by everyone and so we had plenty of opportunities. Everyone we met was extremely polite, if openly curious, about us. This doesn't happen so much in the towns and on the trekking routes where the people are more used to tourists and *Namaste* is tossed carelessly over the shoulder if spoken at all. Indeed you are lucky to get the accompanying palms of the hands together greeting.

All along the route were purpose-built resting places consisting of a raised stone platform with one or two trees planted in the middle to provide shade. These were often mango trees which have nice big leaves and by the size of the trunks, some of them had been there for hundreds of years, while others were mere saplings, carefully protected with wire mesh, which would provide shade for generations to come. The feeling of timelessness of this, an area rarely visited by Westerners, was beginning to impress itself upon me. It was at one of these resting places that we had our first long stop.

The plan had been for the porters to go on ahead and prepare lunch but in view of the late start we decided to have a quick snack instead and carry on to a village called Kahun where we were to stop the night. Munching our nuts and carefully peeled apples we studied one of the typical homesteads of this area. It stood on its own, quite a good sized house with a thick, thatched roof and the reddish brown mud of the walls beautifully smooth and flat. A few yards away was a rough shelter consisting of a wood and straw roof supported on wooden poles; this was for the buffalo and the goat and close by was a dome-shaped haystack which would provide their winter food. A woman with a toddler tied to her back was washing a large piece of cloth, about the size of a bedspread, in a not quite big enough metal bowl. I looked at the colour of the water, it didn't seem to be getting much cleaner but the location of the house, being quite a way from the nearest village, meant that water would probably have to be carried some distance and had therefore to be used sparingly.

One by one our porters slowly toiled up the hill, their enormous burdens carefully protected with sheets of polythene. Ramsingh was the chief cook and foreman, a stockily built man in his mid thirties with calves of steel. Of the other three, two were called Dhan Bahadur and the third Chitra. One of the Dhans -the one carrying the heaviest load - was the skinniest of them

14 As we approached Gumlek, the village band came out to meet us.

15 The Children of Shree Sahabir School, Gumlek, assembling ready for our welcome.

16 Each and every child presented us with a garland of flowers and the traditional *tika*.

17 Covered in red *tika* and flowers but overwhelmed by our reception.

18 Some of the older village lads.

19 Dhane's father (centre) with some of the villagers outside his house.

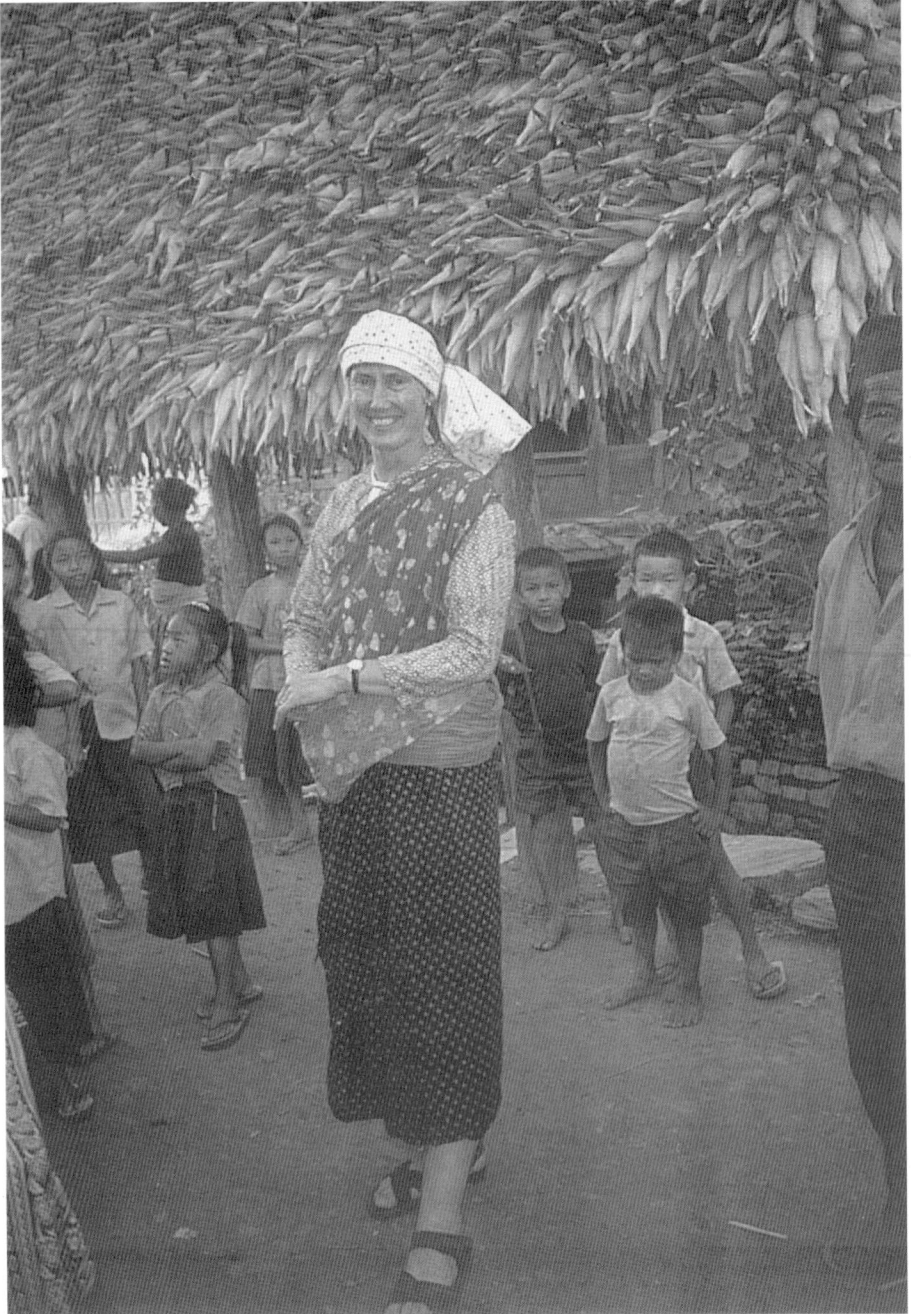

20 Me, dressed in full Nepalese costume.

21 Ramsingh loaded up.

22 Bill and I dressed up ready to plough.

23 Children playing with a stuffed rag football.

24 Ploughing the football field and planting maize seeds.

25 One of the fascinating wind instruments of the village band.

26 The main Street in Gumlek.

all. I'm sure we could have managed with far less gear in order to make their loads lighter. We certainly didn't use the toilet seat or the tent which turned out to have no sides so wasn't considered enough protection against the threatened rain - hence the importance of reaching Kahun before dark. Speaking of toilets, my first experience of a jungle toilet could have ended in disaster.

"I'm just nipping behind this bush" I tossed over my shoulder as I plunged carelessly into a patch of dense undergrowth. Having relieved myself, I stood up to see the ground dropping away sharply about six inches from my feet - one false move and I would have been shooting down an almost sheer drop which had been totally hidden by the thick undergrowth. Bill had obviously sussed out the area a little more carefully than I had.

"You want to be careful, you know, you're not in the Lake District now!" he called, as I returned.

The jungle now opened out and the track levelled off. The rain had stopped, so we had superb views of the hills all around with the typical terraced fields that we had seen in so many photographs and books. We had also read about Nepal's famous leeches and it was at the next resting place that Dhane discovered our first real live leech. These creatures insinuate themselves craftily even through socks and attach themselves to the skin, busily sucking away until they are discovered. I, fortunately, am not squeamish about such things and found them quite a diversion. The only way to detach them is by means of some salt or a lighted cigarette. However, they inject some sort of anti-coagulant into the blood which means that if you take too long to discover them, you can end up with a rather messy, blood-soaked sock.

We were now passing through one or two small villages where the children, far from calling out cheekily as they had done in Pokhara, peeped shyly at us. We decided that some encouragement was needed and bought a packet of sweets to hand out along the way. These were solemnly received with both hands cupped together as is the custom in the villages and particularly in the remote village areas. Higher castes, including ourselves, are supposed to wait until a person of a lower caste greets them first and only then

"Be careful where you go Anne, it's not like the Lake District here, you know!"

may return the greeting. Gifts, such as cigarettes are thrown to a lower caste person and they may not touch or enter the house of someone of a higher caste. Lower castes include blacksmiths, tailors, metalworkers, and even gold and silversmiths. After a while we were able to distinguish them from other castes by their faces which look more Indian than those of the higher castes. Lower caste people are said to 'live for today' and 'enjoy a drink'. This proved to be true in one or two cases when we smelt the local brew, *raksi*, on the breath of one or two of the men we met - at 7.30 in the morning on one occasion! However, I found the caste system difficult to accept and kept having to remind myself to think in a more 'Victorian' way.

Kahun is actually on the top of a hill, higher than the village of Gumlek, and the path began to rise steeply again. It was now late afternoon and children were returning home from school, bag straps round their foreheads. We practised one or two Nepali phrases like *Mero nam Anne ho* and asked them "What is your name?" The girls, in particular, found these attentions extremely embarrassing and giggled shyly behind their hands until one of them bravely found the English words to reply. Our attempts at Nepali were greeted either by puzzled or embarrassed looks showing that they hadn't understood or by a beaming smile and gales of laughter when they had. The changing ex-pressions on the faces of all the Nepalese people we encountered in this area was yet another delightful and fascinating insight into the Nepalese character, adding so much colour and humour to our efforts at verbal communication.

We knew we were nearing the village of Kahun as, on questioning some of the children we met, we learnt that they were from Kahun school, although we could still be anything up to two hours away as children often have a two hour walk to school. We passed the village 'Pub', a wood and straw construc-tion where a dozen or so men and older boys were enjoying a game of cards and a drink of *raksi*. *Raksi* is made by distilling fermented liquid from either millet or soy beans. Each family makes their own brew and consequently the quality varies tremendously. We found the village *raksi* produced in Gumlek to be far superior to the town brew.

As darkness approached we passed more children, engaged on their after school tasks. Some looking like walking haystacks, with big bundles of hay on their backs, others weighed down with *dokos* full of leaves and branches for their buffalo or huge metal water pots full of water. Just as it began to get dark we arrived at a resting place just outside Kahun. Gradually faces appeared out of the gloom and we were soon surrounded by a circle of curious village children. We handed round some of our sweets and exchanged *Namastes*. Two stools were produced for us to sit on and we were given a packet of biscuits each. Dhane introduced one of the women as the wife of one of the Pahar Trust's best carpenters and after some negotiation with the more important people of the village we learned that we had been invited to stay in the village 'community hall'. We were led up to a huge football pitch sized area on one side of which we could just see the school, a high school. On the other side was a large barn-like building where we were to spend the night. Inside were long wooden tables and sturdy wooden chairs. Ramsingh and his gang immediately set to work and within minutes a welcome pot of tea was produced. The tables were pushed together and mattresses laid out on top for us to sleep on - even our sleeping bags were spread out for us.

The building was soon filled with the roaring of the kerosene stoves and the hissing of a huge Tilley lamp and the meal that was produced made all previous meals pale into insignificance. Ramsing certainly knew his stuff and had managed to transform a humble tin of Spam into deliciously spiced cubes accompanied by curried vegetables, rice and *dal*. We had begun the meal with a very tasty vegetable soup and I now realised that in addition to the battery of kitchen equipment, the porters were also carrying many kilos of potatoes, beans, parsnips, apples, bananas, tomatoes and cucumbers, as well as all the rice.

"Finis, Mem Sahib?" was murmured in my ear as our plates were cleared away - I never quite got used to this but was assured it was all part of the porters' British Army training and this was how they addressed the officers and their wives.

All the pots and pans were washed, dried and stacked neatly in regimental order, the sea of faces by the door was shooed away and it was time to settle down for the night. While we were fairly comfortable on our high-rise beds and foam mattresses, the porters merely spread out towels or cloths over the bare concrete floor and lay, spreadeagled, close to the door which was wedged firmly shut with a long wooden pole. After no more than ten minutes the peace was suddenly shattered by a loud explosion, more followed at two or three minute intervals until Dhane, convinced that the village children were up to something, crept out, Gurkha-style, to see what was going on. Hoping to catch whichever child it was who was throwing stones onto the roof, Dhane hid behind a bush in the darkness, but after a few more loud cracks had resounded across the night sky, he decided to climb on the roof to investigate. He caught no children but discovered - nuts! These were falling from a huge tree which was overhanging the roof. The roof, being made of the usual corrugated iron, and the large building providing an echo chamber, resulted in the loud explosive sound when the nuts fell from the tree. After that, nobody got much sleep although the falling nuts did become less frequent. I resorted once more to my earplugs but still could not sleep; my mind was too full of pictures and thoughts of my first day in this unfamiliar, though totally friendly and welcoming, world of the 'real Nepal'. Once in the night I felt the need to relieve myself - too many cups of Ramsingh's tea! Shading my torch, I crept towards the door terrified of tripping over one of the porters' legs. I wrestled with the stake wedging the door but one of the Dhans leapt up and opened it for me, waiting courteously until I returned so that he could wedge it shut again.

Having arrived in the dark I was keen next morning to survey our surroundings. We seemed to be perched on the top of a hill, the school on the opposite side of the football pitch was a long low building raised up on a bank quite a few metres higher than the surroundings. This was one of the two local high schools serving the area and was in fact the school Dhane had attended as a child as there had been no school in Gumlek when he was young. This village was also wanting a new secondary school but the policy of the Pahar Trust ensures that villagers wanting a school have to prove themselves to be well organised and well motivated with a strong and united village committee and good leadership in order to be able to carry the project through. Upon further acquaintance with the village we learned that this was not so. Kahun, being a larger and more scattered village with a greater proportion of low-caste inhabitants, had not got the solidarity and strong leadership that Gumlek most certainly has. Nevertheless, we were treated like VIPs. The special First Aid

Bombarded by - would you believe - nuts!

post toilet was unlocked for us and we were greeted formally by all the important members of the village, and shown the house they had built for a French lady VSO worker who had come to teach at the school some years ago and had stayed for three years. Possibly this was a hint to Bill and me - we soon learnt that when Nepalis give they usually expect something in return!

After a rather rudimentary wash, as the village water supply had dwindled to a trickle, we breakfasted on cheese omelette and set off for Gumlek. The path now led first downwards through fields of rice and millet and then, after crossing a small stream, upwards again through more jungle. This area was very familiar to Dhane who recounted various incidents from his boyhood including one when he had had to shoot a tiger which had attacked one of his goats. There is a tiger trap just outside Gumlek and we were assured that mountain tigers still occasionally come into the villages when food is in short supply. Coincidentally, a few days after our return I heard on the news that a tiger had been attacking villages near Kathmandu and had killed about twenty children before it was finally caught. Dhane had also learned, at an early age, the skills of spear throwing and used to go regularly with his father and brothers on bear hunts. The black bear, which lives in the more inaccessible parts of the jungle, can be very ferocious and will attack humans, whereas the mountain tiger can be frightened away.

After a while Dhane gave a loud hallooing call which echoed through the jungle and was answered by first one voice and then another and another getting further and further away. He said he was calling to the porters ahead to make sure they were going the right way but he later told us that this had been a signal, picked up by various villagers placed at strategic points along the route, that our arrival was imminent! Here too, as we neared the village, the path had been cleared for us and slashed off stalks lay at the side of the track. A fine rain had started to fall and we were offered the shelter of someone's goat shed. Here we sat for some considerable time, chatting to the owner of the goat shed and another of Dhane's friends-and-relations who was home on leave from the Indian army. This, we learned later, was yet another delaying tactic! Finally Dhane said we should make a move and we carried on until we reached a point just outside the village. From here we could see people descending the hill from the nearby village of Bhirkot. One of them was carrying a *madal*, a drum similar to the one Tom had given the school when we first joined the Pahar Trust and another wielded a huge horn bent round in a circle which we also recognised from photographs as being a traditional Nepalese instrument. Yet another short wait was requested while the band assembled and then we heard them coming nearer and nearer. Finally rounding the bend and moving towards us came the full band, a cacophony of rhythmic drumbeats and raucous hooting to the accompaniment of a background drone from a reeded oboe-like instrument. The band was followed by a long trail of villagers who greeted us one by one with garlands of flowers, beginning with Jeet, the headmaster of the school and his father. Older boys of the village then followed, each giving us a small bunch of flowers. Totally overwhelmed and feeling like real celebrities we then had to lead the whole party up to the village, the band following behind still playing loudly. The next hour or so passed in an absolute blur of colour, flowers and welcoming smiles.

Chapter 5 - GUMLEK

We reached the centre of the village where more garlands were presented and the traditional red *tika* powder was pressed onto our foreheads by each of the important members of the village. A large wooden table had been spread with a coloured cloth and two large wooden 'thrones' were draped with more cloths and cushions where we were invited to sit down. By now the sun had come out and after yet more greetings and introductions we sat down gratefully, hoping to have a brief respite from the limelight. Ramsingh brought us a welcome drink of lemon juice and we were offered bananas and yoghurt by the villagers. However, all was not over yet as the band had now assembled in front of us. The dancer had begun his performance and was enticing us to join in. Totally caught up in the festivities we did our best to trip the light fantastic, feeling very clumsy in our walking boots. The tradition, apparently, was to put money in the dancer's hair after the performance and this we did - most of it ending up on the ground as he danced on. By now the whole village seemed to have gathered and after the dancing had finished we surveyed the sea of faces around us. Dhane intimated that we should do a sort of walkabout. One of the mothers was anxious that her little boy, who was immobilised by a plaster cast on one leg which reached up to his waist, should meet us. He had a garland for us and it turned out that he had fallen off a rooftop and broken his hip. The nearest hospital was at Pokhara so he had had to survive being carried down through the jungle to Damauli and then the bumpy bus ride to Pokhara in order to be treated.

Being players of musical instruments ourselves - Bill plays saxophone and I play trombone - we were keen to have a go on some of the band instruments. The horn proved surprisingly difficult to blow, as did another interesting looking instrument with a double reed similar to an oboe.

A group of lads who looked about twelve or thirteen but who turned out to be sixteen and seventeen were eager to practice their English on us. This was quite good as they were all from either Bhirkot or Kahun, the two nearest high schools. Some of the older ones had finished at school and were awaiting the results of their exams. I approached a group of girls but they turned shyly away and Dhane later told us that they had never been to school and so had not learnt any English. It gradually dawned on me that here the education of boys is still regarded as more important than that of girls who are kept very much in the background. The women spend their time working in the fields or at home and are, for the most part, very shy and retiring. In our later conversations with the villagers, it was always the boys and men that were keen to talk to us, being much more confident and outgoing due to their superior education and position in society. The only women I really started to get to know in the short time we were there were Dhane's mother, a lovely warm and lively person, who, being Dhane's mother, had some status in the village; and the leader of a group of 'professional' dancers who came to entertain us the next day. However, I digress. Significant movement and organisation were taking place further up the village and we were ushered back to our 'thrones' again. There followed a ceremony which was for me one of the most emotional and touching parts of our visit. All the school children were arranged in two lines, one of boys and one of girls, the leaders making an arch with two crossed flags -the school flag and the national Nepalese flag. With much shepherding and encouragement by teachers and older boys they marched towards us, each with a beautiful garland of flowers they had made themselves, and one by one they carefully placed the garlands around our necks and smeared our foreheads with red *tika* powder from a tray on the table. *Namastes* were exchanged with each and every child, some of whom were so tiny they had to be lifted up to reach us. Some of the garlands had ended up a tangled mass of flowers and wouldn't fit over our heads but we received them just as gratefully and piled them up on the table in front of us. Totally overwhelmed by such attentions I dared not speak and the memory of the occasion can still bring tears to my eyes. Now covered in red powder and flowers - I was pleased I was wearing a red T-shirt - Bill made a short speech of thanks, translated by Dhane and, the formalities over, we handed round the remainder of our sweets to the children. Some of these were blackcurrant and liquorice brought from home and for the rest of the day we were to come across groups of little children peering fascinatedly through the purple wrappers!

While all this had been going on Ramsingh and the other porters had set themselves up on the ground floor of Dhane's parents' house, their groundsheet and equipment taking up half the floor area. They were anxious for us to eat the meal they had prepared and we retired gratefully to the dark interior of the house where we dined on a delicious chicken which had been donated by the village.

The 'party night' Tom had talked to us about was due to start that evening and, feeling very hot and sweaty after our walk and my face absolutely covered in *tika* powder I decided to brave the curious stares and take a shower, Nepalese style. This involved going to the village tap, soap and towel in hand, hoisting my skirt up under my armpits, removing T-shirt and underclothes and then trying to wash all over underneath the skirt, without showing anything above mid-calf level! This was a difficult operation at the best of times but made more so by the audience of villagers waiting patiently to fill their water pots while I splashed about ineptly. I stuck to my guns, however, and finally retired, skirt dripping, to the privacy of Dhane's younger brother's bedroom, which he had kindly lent us during our stay in the village, in order to dry off and change my clothes. It would definitely not have been the done thing to strip off even down to a swimming costume in this or any of the villages where the Hindu religion is very strong and traditions die hard. Even on the popular trekking routes, while shorts and trousers are becoming more acceptable, anything briefer is likely to offend. Men, of course, can get away with merely keeping their underpants on.

Refreshed, and temporarily out of the limelight, we took a stroll down the village. It was as if time had stood still for about seven hundred years. A raised 'crazy paving' path led down the centre of the village, this was to keep a dry 'main street' during the monsoon. On either side were large two and three storey houses with reddish brown brick walls and slate or thatched roofs, many of which had pumpkins growing on them, their huge green leaves twining up the walls and sprawling over the roof tops. Further back were smaller houses with only one storey; they were of wood and mud construction, with neat thatched roofs. The bigger houses boasted wooden balconies and strong wooden shutters to the windows while the windows of the smaller houses were open to the elements. Each house had its own open-sided goat or buffalo shed, again wooden and thatched. Buffaloes are very much a sign of wealth and status in the villages and to own two pairs is a bit like being a two car family. They are used for ploughing, meat and for their milk which surprised me as I thought that goat's milk would be more popular. However, buffalo milk is thought to be far superior and goats are kept mainly for their meat. Another sign of status and wealth is the size of the dried maize stack. The drying cobs of maize are hung from a high wooden framework suspended between two poles and they can be as high as twelve to fifteen feet.

Inside, the houses have hard mud floors and in the case of Dhane's family house the main room was quite large - about twenty feet by twelve feet and simply furnished with a wooden table and two benches. In one of the corners, which had not been taken over by Ramsingh's equipment, stood two of the large metal water pots that we had seen in great quantity in towns and villages alike. These were made of brass but they can also be of copper or aluminium. They are between two and three feet tall, wide and cylindrical at the bottom with a narrow neck and a wider flat lip. I would have loved to bring one home with me but didn't think I would get away with it as hand luggage on the plane, so I had to be content with one of the smaller brass drinking vessels purchased later on in Kathmandu. Also in the room was a huge wide copper bowl some twenty inches across which was used to catch rain water. Off the main room was the kitchen which was about half the size with a hollowed out floor area at one side which was the fireplace. Although nearly all of the cooking is done on wood fires there are no chimneys in village houses. Presumably these would be difficult to construct and would let in the rain during the monsoon. The fire is also the main source of warmth in the winter; kerosene, which has to be carried up from Damauli, a good day's walk away, is used mainly for lamps. Strung across the kitchen was a hammock where Dhane's sister-in-law rocked her baby to sleep.

The baby was a beautiful sturdy little girl who brought out all my maternal instincts as I sat with her in my lap later on in the afternoon. Forgetting that of course Nepalese babies don't wear nappies, my newly washed skirt was soon wet through! Access to the upper storey was by means of an outside wooden staircase which led from the lower verandah to the upper balcony. Four or five small bedrooms opened onto this balcony and ours was at the end. It had one side with windows the full length, making it very light and cool during the daytime. It was so warm at night that there was no need for shutters and the other bedrooms with only one window at the end would be more for winter use. This house also boasted its own earth closet situated discreetly at the back of the house and carefully padlocked against unauthorised users. As guests we were permitted to use this fairly palatial convenience which was a wooden slatted construction about six feet square with a wooden boarded floor in the centre of which was cut a neat square hole. Yards below was a deep pit which would take years to fill and from which there was no smell at all. The villagers were very discreet about their toilet arrangements. Certain areas in the village were designated as toilet areas and if the area was in use the next person would retire gracefully round the corner and wait, out of sight, for the user to emerge - I never once saw a Nepali over the age of about five relieve himself in any of the villages. This, of course, was not true of the towns and trekking areas although it did not occur as frequently as one might have expected.

At present this area of Nepal is sparsely populated so there is not the need for the conservationist measures that have had to be taken in the trekking areas. The village takes only what it needs from the environment and every-thing they use, they are able to make themselves. Rush mats are made from the maize leaves and stalks, as are the small round mats or *chakati* for sitting on. Hand brushes are also made from dried stems, thatch from the rice straw and wood for ploughs, tools and frameworks for buildings is all from the surrounding forests. Bricks are handmade from the local red clayish mud and they even use toothpaste made from a crushed up red stone found in nearby streams. Only the slate for the roofs has to be carried up from the valley. Cloth is woven in some of the villages and a tailor travels round from village to village taking orders and completing work before moving on to the next village.

Further down the village, in a small courtyard between some houses, a lively football game was going on amongst some young boys. The ball was made of cloth stuffed with more soft material which was much more comfort-able on the bare-footed players than a leather or plastic one would have been. Bill and Dhane joined in with gusto while I watched, afraid that the bare feet would be trodden on by their big boots. My fears were unjustified however as they were skilful enough to jump nimbly out of the way. On all the occasions when we saw children playing, the girls and boys always played separately, the boys preferring football, volleyball or a rather rougher version of 'tig' while the girls were more often seen playing fivestones or skipping, often while minding a younger brother or sister by carrying them on their backs.

Walking back up the village we were invited to see the goat which had been especially killed for that evening's meal. Thankfully, most of the dismembering had already been done and the 'butcher' was carefully sorting out the various parts of the carcass and weighing them on a hand held balance.

If we had been hoping for a peaceful afternoon before the evening's festivities we were quite wrong as we were now about to entertain the village with our efforts at learning how to plough. Bill was dragged off one way and I another to be first of all dressed up in traditional Nepalese costume. Bill's consisted of a *dhoti*†, a skimpy piece of cloth, which barely reached his knees and which was wrapped round his waist and tucked in. Mine however, was a lot more complicated. First the *guni*, a piece of material about five metres long, which was wound round my waist by a group of enthusiastic women under the direction of Dhane's mother. The middle section was then folded into a number of pleats at the front which were then bunched together and tied to the first corner. The remaining two metres or so was then wrapped round once more and tucked in the back; here much adjustment had to be made and extra material pulled out from the pleated bit as I was about a foot taller than the average Nepali woman.

I then had to squeeze myself into the closely fitting top called a *cholo*, the long sleeves of which reached just past my elbow. Then to round it all off another long but narrower piece of material was wound several times round my waist fairly tightly and again tucked in at the back - this is called the *patuka*. I tried to memorise all this so that I could show the children back at school in England. The *guni* is in actual fact worn in a similar way to the Indian sari - also worn by Nepalese town dwellers - the only difference being that the last two metres or so is wound again round the waist instead of being worn over

---

† I later discovered that the village version of this garment is more often a *kachhad* and is longer than a *dhoti* which is worn more in the Terai region.

the left shoulder as with the sari. The whole outfit felt very bulky especially with this huge thickness of material round the waist and I later asked Dhane to explain why they needed all this material just to hold up the *guni*. Surely it must be very hot working in the sunshine in all this lot? He explained that the purpose of the *patuka* is not only to hold up the *guni* and make sure that no bare skin shows beneath the *cholo* but it also acts as a support for the back and a rest for the *doko*. For women who work long and back-breaking hours tending their crops and carrying heavy loads, often with a child on their backs all day as well, the strain on the back must be tremendous and this support must be essential especially after three or four pregnancies. Certainly all the women over the age of about thirty wear the *patuka* all day and sometimes sleep in it. Even the way the *guni* is worn is designed specially to fit in with the lifestyle. Nepalese women do not wear underwear and the *cholo* is close-fitting, giving some support to the breasts. The *guni* is tight at the back so that when the women squat down (either on the ground or up in trees when they are collecting fodder) they do not expose their nether regions, while the fullness is all at the front to allow greater ease of movement when walking. To complete the costume I was given a scarf to wind round my head in whatever way I chose and a necklace of thin shiny yellow strings of beads. Somebody tried to squeeze some coloured bangles over my large hand but gave up, realising that they might not get them off again!

Suitably clad, we were then each presented with a *hacia*, a curved reaping knife in a wooden holster, to be tied round the waist with string, and over my shoulder was tied a cloth inside which I was to keep the maize seeds. The field we were to plough was actually the levelled site of the new school and the money from the sale of the crop to be planted was to go towards the school building. After a brief lesson from the ploughman, Bill took over the two buffaloes which had first been muzzled just in case they took a dislike to their new driver. The idea was to lean heavily on the plough as it was pulled along between the buffaloes and try and keep a straight furrow at the same time. My job was dead easy - all I had to do was follow behind, dropping the seed into the furrow at intervals. The trickiest bit was turning the buffaloes at the end of the field. They seemed to know what they were doing though and obediently turned round when Bill lifted the plough and swung it round through one hundred and eighty degrees. Eyeing the not quite straight furrows, the real ploughman decided that we had messed up his neat rows quite enough and we took a bow to a round of applause from the amused villagers.

We wondered what other tricks the villagers had up their sleeves but were assured by Dhane that we were to be entertained by the children later that evening but first of all Bill, along with several other visiting dignitaries, would be asked to make a speech.

Chapter 6 - PARTY TIME

For our evening meal Ramsingh had prepared one of his specialities. This was a dish called *mo-mo* which was meat balls in neat little pastry-like parcels which were then steamed. In order to achieve the finely ground meat necessary for this dish the cooks must have spent hours chopping all the meat and vegetables with just a long bladed knife. I made a mental note to search out my old mincer and bring it over on our next visit. The *mo-mo* were delicious and we were offered some of Dhane's mum's home-brewed *raksi* to wash it down. This tasted a little like whisky but was colourless and not as strong and to my inexperienced taste buds, not being a whisky drinker, was a lot smoother. Meanwhile, outside the festivities had begun. More chairs had been brought out for some VIPs who had arrived from neighbouring villages. We were introduced to Kesh, the area hill village selection officer for the British Gurkhas. He had come from the nearby village of Bhirkot which we were supposed to be visiting the next day. He was a charming man whom we were to get to know quite well over the next couple of days. His English was pretty good too which made communication a lot easier. Various other important officials were introduced to us and shortly some plates of goat meat were brought for us to sample.

By now it was quite dark but Gumlek has an ingenious electricity supply from a large battery which is re-charged daily by solar energy. It somehow converts to 240 volts and supplies enough power for two or three portable fluorescent tube lights, each about a foot long. We understood that the brain power behind this was Jeet, the headmaster, with a little help from Dhane, when he was there, for he was an electrician in the British army. This source of power was also used to supply the PA system which was used later down at the school for the speeches and folk dancing.

Glancing round the group of villagers sitting nearest to us, I appeared to be the only female, and this was to be the case on several subsequent occasions. The reason for this, of course, was that the Nepalese women were all far too busy slaving away in the kitchen to have time to sit around idly chatting. I don't think the villagers quite knew what to make of me but they must have known that the position of western women in society is different from that of their women. I was treated in exactly the same way as Bill and expected to take an equal share in all the formalities and ceremonies. I would really have to get to grips with the Nepali language if I wanted to talk to the women.

I did not notice what time it was when the signal came from the school some five hundred yards away that they were ready to start and we all picked our way through the darkness to the present school 'playground' at the end of which was a raised 'stage' complete with electric lighting and PA system. There must have been more than just Gumlek village there as some two to three hundred people were already gathered and sitting patiently on the ground. This was to be quite a formal occasion and all the visiting dignitaries made speeches in Nepali before Bill was invited to make his. Being a head-master and well used to speaking in school assemblies and at parents' meet-ings, he spoke confidently, if a little formally though this, we were assured, was what the occasion demanded. He thanked the village for our welcome, explained who we were and the purpose of our visit and said how he was looking forward to meeting all the school children the next day. The main problem was remembering to break the speech down into short enough chunks for Dhane to translate. Dhane himself was totally relaxed and self-as-sured and was obviously held in very high regard by the whole village. I thought I would get away without having to say anything but I was not allowed to escape, and, totally unprepared, I mounted the stage and faced the sea of faces. Bill had already said all there was to say so I merely re-iterated my thanks for the wonderful welcome and then ran out of things to say.

Just as it was time for the folk dancing to begin it started to rain, this soon worsened into a steady downpour which threatened to disrupt the whole evening. However, the show went on while the audience sat under all manner of makeshift shelters. Pieces of cloth, scarves, polythene, tarpaulins and a few umbrellas appeared while we flattened ourselves against the school wall in an effort to shelter under the overhanging roof. The children must have spent many hours practising the dances that they performed. Each one told a story, some about love between two people who lived far away from each other, some about their family life working in the fields, some about a man who loved a woman who didn't care for him or vice-versa. At the end of each dance we and the other visitors were invited to pledge a sum of money for whichever dance we liked best. This of course was a very difficult decision, as all the dances, performed by young and old, were charming and the costumes extremely colourful. The dancing of the men and boys was particularly light and nimble, almost dainty but without being at all effeminate. Nepalese men are very slightly built and so this style of dancing suits them - I can't imagine the typical British male being able to carry it off! The style of the girls' dancing was very graceful and flowing, typifying the Nepalese woman's modest demeanour.

Well, here we were in the middle of the jungle, watching live theatre in the pouring rain! The performance carried on until 2 o'clock in the morning by which time we were soaked to the skin but not at all cold, the rain being more like a continuous warm shower. Eventually, the villager under whose umbrella I had been sitting said

"Home go, I take umbrella?"

"*Danyabad*," I thanked him and we splashed back up the muddy path to the village, stripped off our wet clothes and crawled gratefully into our beds.

The next day I awoke early to the sound of cockerels crowing. The smell of wood smoke drifted up from below and although it was only 5.30 am the village was awake and the day had begun. I looked out of the window, the sun was up and everything was bathed in an unreal golden light. A few houses down a woman was washing at the tap. I studied her technique. She seemed to have her *guni* tucked up under her armpits and she stood under the tap and first washed her hair, then using the *guni* as a sort of giant flannel, she gave herself a good swab down all over. She then put a long dress over her head and pulled the skirt down to her ankles and hauled the soaking wet *guni* out from underneath. Very efficient, I thought, and all without resorting to a towel. This was obviously something I needed to practice.

After breakfast the very important ceremony of laying the foundation stone to the new school was to take place. Dhane, as site manager-cum-civil engineer, was in charge and we all walked down to the newly levelled site, closely followed by the visiting dignitaries who had stayed overnight in the village. We had been too busy concentrating on our ploughing the day before to really take in the surroundings but today we could see that a huge area had already been levelled. Four PTN (Pahar Trust, Nepal) wheelbarrows were stood at the side and I contemplated what a mammoth task it must have been to level such a huge area using only hand shovels and wheelbarrows. The levelled area was to be the football pitch and was half ploughed, ready for its winter crop. The school itself was to be built behind this area on a piece of higher ground which had already been planted out with a millet crop. It was here that the corner of the building was to be marked and the foundation stone laid.

"We use the 3-4-5 method to make a right angle" announced Dhane, producing a ball of string. I racked my brains, we had a long tape measure but no set square and after the first bit of measuring and knot-tying I realised that the 3-4-5 method was the good old square on the hypotenuse (3 squared plus 4 squared equals 5 squared). This age-old method of constructing a right-angle had been used by the ancient Egyptians when building the pyramids so why not now? The right angle having been constructed by making knots in the string exactly three, four and five inches apart, the corner was then marked with a stick in the ground and the two sides extended the full length and width of the school and marked with string. It was at this corner that the foundation stone was to be laid. A visiting priest had come especially to conduct the ceremony. He was a member of the highest Hindu caste, the *Brahmins,* which is the only caste allowed to be a Hindu priest. (Although it was a sweltering hot day, he spent the whole time wearing a thick, heavy pullover while everyone else was in T-shirts, so whether this was something to do with his priestliness or not, I don't know.)

The ceremony began with first Bill and I, then all the village committee members in turn digging out a shovel or two of earth from the marked corner of the site. The priest then brought a tray which held some red *tika* powder, some rice, flowers, incense sticks and a small oil lamp. He placed the flowers and the oil lamp in the bottom of the hole and said a few words while throwing in some rice dyed red with the *tika.* He then lit the oil lamp and the incense sticks. We were all then invited to throw on more flowers and grains of rice. The rice and flowers were gifts to the gods and the lighted lamp was to ensure the strength and endurance of the building. Finally Bill lifted up a flat slab of stone and placed it over the hole and all its contents and then the priest blessed everyone in the traditional Hindu way with rice and *tika* pressed onto our foreheads. Walking back to the village I wondered how long it would be before we could return and find the school complete. We had, in less than a year, already raised two and a half thousand of the eight or nine thousand pounds needed to complete the school but our task of raising the money was easy compared to theirs. All the sand for the cement and aggregate had to be carried up in *dokos* from the river bed which was a day's walk away and all the work to be done on the school was in addition to the normal full day's work looking after their crops and animals. Surely we were looking at six or seven years' work? I only hoped that the motivation could be sustained until the building was complete.

We walked back to the present school where the formal exchange of flags and the presenting of our gifts was to take place. This was a long low stone building with very small classrooms which were also dark because of the small windows on one side only. The roof was of corrugated iron, making the rooms very noisy during the monsoon. Inside the classrooms were long tables with benches behind them where as many as forty-five children would be all squashed together. Today the children formed an avenue - girls on one side and boys on the other - across the middle of the playground and they all clapped as we walked down the middle. They were then marched, military-style, into shorter rows spreading across the playground where they sat down and looked up at us expectantly. Bill then handed the gifts we had brought, one at a time, to Jeet with a few words of explanation about each, Dhane again acting as translator. We had brought as much as our airline baggage allowance would permit; including more serious things such as an atlas, an inflatable globe, books, pencils, crayons, stamps, coins, photos of our school and all the children and a recorder, as well as some fun things like a reel of red ribbon for the girls' hair, a football, models of a London bus and a tractor, some school caps, a Grimsby Town football scarf, and a couple of sets of juggling balls which caused great amusement when Bill demonstrated with them. I was pleased I had rushed to finish making our school flag ready to bring with us as the formal exchanging of school flags was the most important part of the ceremony. Ours was burgundy with the school emblem of an owl appliquéd on in blue fabric and a tiny Union Jack in the corner. Gumlek, or Shree Sahabir school as it was called, gave us their flag which was green with a six pointed star painted in the middle which is the symbol for all schools in Nepal and an open book at the bottom, together with the name of the school in English and Nepali.

I had opened my big mouth earlier and suggested that the children might like to learn an English song, thinking that I could slip quietly into one of the classrooms and teach it to just a small group. What I was not prepared for was Dhane expecting me to sing 'If you're happy and you know it, clap your hands' in front of all these people.

"What now?"

"Yes, you sing, I make them join in."

Taking a deep breath, I launched into the song. It must have sounded very strange to them as their style of singing is totally different to ours and not even based on the diatonic scale. However, encouraged by Dhane they all joined in the clapping and foot stamping and we all had a good laugh.

We had brought some ballpoint pens with us with the names of the two schools stamped on in gold lettering and these we now handed out to the children who were there, about seventy or eighty of them, although the number of children on roll was considerably more - about a hundred and sixty. As I have mentioned earlier, full attendance is never possible in the village schools where children are so often needed to help work in the fields. This was particularly true of this time of the year as it was the beginning of the rice harvest. The children were delighted with these pens and wore them proudly, clipped into their shirt pockets or, in the case of the girls, tucked into their hair.

There followed a photo session with pictures of the whole school, older ones at the back holding up the flag and some smaller children at the front wearing our school baseball caps which looked huge on them - Nepalese children are a lot smaller than their western counterparts. We left them enjoying a game of volleyball with the new net which had been given to them by a returning Gurkha soldier. I found myself thinking of all the things we had back at school in England which we no longer used which would be so much appreciated here, where the school had so little. Old reading books, charts, PE equipment could all be utilised - it might even be possible to rig up one of our out of date computers to their electric battery. How wasteful we are with paper and pencils, throwing sheets and sheets of paper away just because they haven't photocopied just right and discarding pencils when they get too short. If we could supply exercise books and paper for the new school, more pupils would be encouraged to come regularly as families have to supply their own exercise books for their children, expensive items which have to be bought in the nearest town. Dhane told us that when he was studying as a boy his family couldn't afford all the paper and exercise books he needed so he used old newspapers, writing over the print in the opposite direction with a darker coloured pen.

We were beginning to feel the strain of this action-packed visit and we both fell asleep for an hour after lunch. We were awakened by the sound of drums being beaten and vocal chords exercised and, looking over the balcony, we saw that the five female dancers who had come from a neighbouring village were getting ready to begin their performance. Sawdust was being carefully sprinkled over the ground by two young boys to soak up the few puddles that remained from the morning's brief shower of rain and a white canopy had been stretched over the dancing area as a further precaution. At the other end rush mats had been spread on the ground for the drummers and wooden chairs placed behind for the visitors. These five dancers were aged between about seventeen and twenty-five and were all very attractive, as are all young Nepalese women until they reach about thirty-five or forty years when they seem suddenly to age. They had never been to school and had chosen to train as dancers instead. Each village or small group of villages has its own particular dance and today's dancing was different from the folk dancing we had seen the day before which is a more national type of dance. It was different in that it was less varied and tended to follow the same basic rhythm beaten out by the drums but was no less graceful and, especially when it came to the men's dances, was more repetitive and tribal in nature. Each dance began with a loud wailing cry from one of the group of men and boys who were seated on the rush mats, with a *kainjadi*, a single sided drum, made from the skin of the monitor lizard. This skin is very much sought after and quite large sums of money are paid for an intact lizard skin. The drum beat was then taken up by the rest of the drummers. This was a basic four beats to the bar rhythm with the accent on the first beat which was played with the flat of the hand in the centre of the drum to produce a loud but 'flat' sound. The following quicker beats were played nearer the rim with splayed fingers. This is the rhythm, as near as I can get, written in conventional musical notation:-

1 - and - 2 - and - 3   1 - and - 2 - and - 3

As we joined the audience, we were each given a *kainjadi* so we could join in the drumming. It wasn't long, however, before the leader of the dancers was beckoning to us to join in the dancing. Once again realising that we weren't going to get away with non-participation, we obliged. The men's dance was very energetic, involving Russian-style squat jumps which Bill's un-practised knee joints weren't quite up to. The women's dance, however, was less hectic and I managed to pick up the basic step.

One of the dancers then lent me her bells to try. These were inside a hollow ring of quite heavy metal which went round the ankle and attached to the middle toe with tape. A regular rhythm was then kept up by slightly stamping with the foot that wore the bells. When combined with the graceful arm movement, this was actually quite a nice dance to do. A group of women must have sensed my enthusiasm because they then dragged me off to put on all the traditional gear again. I joined in once more but realised I would need a lot more practice to become as expert as they were. I would also need to develop the hard patches on my ankles that the dancers had from wearing the heavy rings of bells!

Before we were allowed to sit down they each planted a 'kiss' on our cheeks which turned out to be quite a sharp bite! Normally, the Nepalese do not show any kind of affection or intimacy in public even between husband and wife, although it is quite common to see men with their arms round each others' shoulders although only in a companionable sort of way as Dhane assured us that homosexuality is unheard of in Nepal.

Doing our best with the Nepalese dancing

The dancers were tireless and we could still hear the regular drumbeat as darkness fell and we retired once more to Dhane's mother's ground floor for our evening meal. Villagers too were drifting off and returning later, presumably after they had eaten. Certainly most of the audience was male, so the wives must have been busy preparing the meal. The only time a woman is not allowed in the kitchen is at the time of menstruation when she is considered to be unclean and not allowed to touch food. In the villages where the extended family is very much the norm, this is not a problem as there is always a mother or sister to step in, but Dhane, living in Kathmandu and away from his relations, has had to become a competent cook.

I don't know whether it was the effects of a few glasses of *raksi* or mere curiosity but after we had finished eating a group of young lads gradually gathered round us eager both to practice their English and to teach us Nepali. We had mastered *Tapai kosto hunu huncha?* (How are you?) and *Mero nam Anne ho* (my name is Anne) and other phrasebook standards as well as numbers up to ten. However, when it comes to Nepali there are not only many ways of saying the same thing depending on who you are talking to and what the occasion is - formal or informal - but also many dialects and even totally different languages spoken in different villages. Most villages have a village language or dialect and many older members can speak only this and cannot understand other forms of Nepalese. Added to this is the difficult pronunciation of the language which has twelve vowel sounds and forty-six consonant sounds. All these are again pronounced slightly differently even by different members of the same family. This led to a great deal of confusion, earnest faces tried to convince us that his was the right way to say it and peals of good-natured laughter greeted our attempts. Nepalis take education very seriously, it being their only gateway to a better standard of living, and they naturally expected us to be just as serious about learning their language as they contorted their faces into exaggerated mouth and lip movements to try and get us to enunciate to their satisfaction. One lad, an angelic looking curly haired boy of about fifteen was particularly earnest and kept coming back to me later in the evening and the next day.

"I teach you?" he'd smile, and off we'd go again.

The dancing was hotting up again outside and this time it was the turn of the girls to sing and the men to dance. Some of the younger boys set the rhythm going with the *madal,* a cylindrical drum with a skin either end. Here again each village has its own particular rhythm and this was a lot more sophisticated than the one played on the *kainjadi* as I discovered when Dhane tried to teach it to me. The dancing grew more and more energetic as different young men and boys took to the floor, each one trying to outdo the other with his athleticism. As the night wore on, the guests one by one began to set off for their villages. Kesh came to say goodbye and assured us that he and his village of Bhirkot were looking forward to our visit the next day on our way back to Damauli.

The last, and for us probably the most significant, of the ceremonies we took part in was to take place later that evening. Dhane had asked us earlier if Bill would like to adopt Jeet the headmaster as a 'brother' in Nepal. This would be both an honour for Jeet and his family and a more personal way of cementing the link between ourselves and Gumlek, this village which, in just two days, we had come to love. We agreed that this was a great idea and the ceremony would mean that Jeet would become Bill's *mit* or brother and his parents would regard Bill as their adopted son. From then on Bill could only refer to Jeet as *mit* and to his wife as *mitini* and vice versa. It would mean that whenever we visited Nepal we would always be able to stay with Jeet's parents and would be treated by them in the same way as their own son. I was not quite sure how this would work the other way around but obviously if Jeet ever came to England he would be most welcome to stay with us. One of the rather odd and somewhat contradictory aspects of this new relationship was that there was now to be no physical contact between Jeet and myself or between Bill and Jeet's wife who was called Gali - we weren't even allowed to sit on the same bench as each other. The only reason for this that I can think of is to preclude any possibility of each man running off with his *mit's* wife - I shall have to question Dhane further on this when I get the chance‡. It is in fact possible for Nepalese men to have more than one wife and we were told that Jeet's father had another wife, though we never met her. Jeet's father was

‡ Dhane assured me that physical contact is not the custom in Nepal so this non-contact is just part of the tradition.

a real character, himself a retired Gurkha who had served in the Second World War and who proudly showed us a war wound on his chest.

The ceremony involved the exchange of Nepalese and English money. Jeet did a bit better out of this as we didn't have a pound coin, which would have been the equivalent of the one hundred rupee note given to Bill, who had to give Jeet a fiver! However, this money is a token of the friendship and is to be kept safe for the duration of the relationship which should be until death.

There followed the usual garlands and *tika* and offerings of bananas and apples to us. My eyes searched round for Jeet's wife who was now my adopted sister-in-law but she had hurried away into the shadows. Dhane explained that she was a particularly shy person and I vowed once more to try and perfect my Nepali so that I could get to know her.

Chapter 7 - GOODBYE

We had to make an early start the next day as the route back to Damauli was to be a longer river route and we also had to fit in our visit to Bhirkot. The partying carried on after we had gone to bed and there was even someone drumming when we awoke next morning! All our plans for an early start, however, were dashed by a heavy fall of rain. The gifts that the villagers had made for us were also not quite finished as everyone had been too busy dancing the night before. Finally the sun came out and we were able to take some photos of our newly adopted family and of Dhane's family who had been so hospitable - Dhane's mother had put on a lovely yellow sari for the photo and I shall always remember her with great fondness. Just before we set off a group of young men came forward with the gifts they had made for the school. These included a small replica of the wooden 'planer' used to flatten the furrows after they had been ploughed, two wooden replicas of the curved reaping knives each in a beautiful carved sheath one of which was for Bill personally, and two specially made *kainjadis* one of which was for the school and the other for Tom Langridge. The paint was still wet on the drums as they had only been finished that morning!

It was time for farewells as we were behind schedule because of the rain. The porters had already set off and, wearing the last two garlands, we sadly waved goodbye to everyone, promising to carry on raising the money for their school and to return and see them again before too long. We walked under a specially made banner saying "Goodbye, see you again". Some of the villagers followed us to the outskirts of the village where we had met the band on our arrival which now seemed ages ago. Our minds still full of the events of the past three days, we walked the few kilometres to Bhirkot in the now very humid atmosphere. Kesh was waiting for us and showed us round the village including the school. This was a high school, and for some reason the roof space was open all the way along. As there were no ceilings this meant that the dividing walls between the classrooms ended at a height of about seven feet. This must have caused tremendous problems of concentration for pupils and teachers as each class must have had to shut out the noise from the two classes either side of it at least. Kesh then took us to a viewpoint looking south. We could see the whole of the valley below and the Kali Gandaki river winding its way beneath us. On the other side of the river the hills rose again before dropping down to the Terai region beyond. We were looking down at one of the few crossing points of this river and this is only possible for a few weeks of the year during the dry season when it is low enough to be crossed by boat. At all other times it is too wide and too fast flowing. The Kali Gandaki is a sacred river and therefore very important to the Nepalese and a bridge, Kesh explained, would make a tremendous difference to the people of the area, not only facilitating easier trade and communication but also enabling families to visit each other and even members of the same family to visit relations that they perhaps hadn't seen for years. Talking to Dhane later about this, he said that the cost of a metal suspension footbridge, similar to the one we had crossed in Damauli would be in the region of thirty to forty thousand pounds. This set our minds working. What a fantastic project this would be for a town or borough council in the UK to take on! We were talking about less than the cost of an average house which was surely an achievable target for even a small town to raise.

Returning to the village we were proudly shown the statue of a Hindu god that one of Kesh's sons was sculpting with a cement like material on a metal framework. He too was trying to get into the British Gurkhas but had to undergo the same selection process as all the others - no nepotism here!

Before we left, Bill was presented with a silver tiepin representing the Gurkha symbol of two crossed Gurkha knives. This was indeed a great honour and, prompted by Dhane that something was expected in return, we made a donation of one thousand rupees. This donation was to go towards the building of a new temple in the village, a project being undertaken by a group of older women called the Ama party. Each village has such a committee comprising the older and more influential women of the village and they take on projects of particular interest to the women of the village while the more important decisions are made by the village committee which is strictly men only. As religion plays a very important part in the lives of all Hindus, particularly the women, the upkeep of the village temples is always high on their list of priorities.

The original plan to return to Damauli by the river route had been abandoned because of heavy rainfall which had made the track very slippery and the river uncrossable in places. We were now going to return via Kahun and back to Damauli the way we had come so we left Bhirkot, promising to see Kesh again, as I'm sure we would, especially if we could get someone in England to take on the bridge project. Our path was now a steep uphill climb towards the hilltop village. The porters were ahead of us and had set up a rather late lunch in a clearing in the jungle. Ramsingh's lemon juice was most welcome - I would have to get the recipe from him. The question of where we were to spend the night was discussed and a local who had joined us thought that it could well rain again that night. It was here that we discovered that Chandra's 'tent' had, in fact, got no sides and no groundsheet so if we were camping we were likely to get pretty wet. It was decided to prevail upon the hospitality of Kahun once more and hope that the nuts had all fallen off by now! A message was sent and we arrived later in the afternoon. The village was once again very welcoming and opened up the community hall and the toilet. However, this time they were ready for us and their Ama Party had organised some dancing and a village welcome for us later that evening. We could hear the villagers assembling outside as we were enjoying Ramsing's cuisine, so we came out into the darkness and, by the light of Chandra's Tilley lamp, we were once again presented with garlands and entertained with dances. This time the first dancer was an older woman who was one of the members of the Ama party. Her dancing was no less skilful, however, than that of the two young girls who followed and she was a lot less shy, some of her hand movements and significant looks at Bill being most suggestive! The drummer was a young lad who didn't look more than ten or eleven years old and was very skilful on the *madal*.

The entertainment looked like carrying on for some time, so Dhane, who was talking about a really early start the next morning in order to complete the longish walk to Damauli and catch the last bus to Pokhara, stepped in. It transpired that this Ama party was also collecting money for their Hindu temple and was still hopeful that we could do something to help them build a new school. Bill made a short speech - one old woman at the front was absolutely hanging on every word! - saying that he would mention the school to the Pahar Trust but couldn't make any promises, thanking them for their hospitality and the entertainment and finally giving the Ama party the expected donation towards their temple. I thought that the money could be better spent on a more practical project such as the building of toilets for the school which as yet had no such provision for its five hundred or so pupils, but then I was a mere Westerner with totally different priorities.

I awoke at 5.30 the next morning to the roar of the kerosene stove. I stumbled outside into the early morning mist to get a bit more light in order to put in my contact lenses. Little faces began to appear as I got out various bottles of cleaning solutions and started to clean my lenses before inserting them. In a few minutes quite a crowd had gathered and I don't know what they thought this strange woman was doing to her eyes but when I held out one of the lenses for them to see they backed off, only creeping forward when I turned my back on them again - it was a bit like that game we used to play as kids called Grandmother's Footsteps! Contact lenses firmly in place, I was now able to get a move on and we were packed and away by 7.00. Women and children from the village were ahead of us and already hard at work on their rice harvest. We could hear their voices echoing across the valley sometimes singing, sometimes calling to each other. Several children passed us, loaded up with hay or leaves for their animals, and looking up above the path we saw a woman perched high up in a tree, chopping down the branches with the all-purpose *hacia* or curved reaping knife that everyone carries.

"I take you to typical small villages" explained Dhane. "Here, villagers never see white people."

The villages we now passed through were indeed much smaller and obviously poorer than Gumlek. The houses were smaller and more tightly packed together and there were more of the mud and thatch type with just open holes in the walls for windows than the more elaborate two and three storey balconied houses we had seen in other villages. The children eyed us curiously and backed away at first when we tried to take a photograph. However, an older woman stepped in and organised them into a group for us. Another woman let us photograph her baby who was sitting on the mud floor outside his house, feeding himself with rice from a bowl. The children, their bag straps around their foreheads, were setting off for school and, as the time was only about 8.30 am, must have had quite a walk as school in the

27 Jeet, the headmaster, sporting the Grimsby Town football scarf.

28 Jeet with his family, not forgetting the canary!

29 Bill and I with Dhane's family. . .and 30 below with Jeet's family.

31 The very delightful dancing girls who had come, especially for the occasion, from the neighbouring village of Dubung.

32 The party area outside Dhane's house complete with rainproof awning.

33 The rhythm section!

34 The dancing went on well into the night.

35 Ghurka field surveying, the 3-4-5 method of marking the corner, and 36 below, with the village committee looking on.

37 The cleared site of the new school.

38 Bill digging the first spade-full of the foundations.

39 Dhane's father taking part in the ceremonial digging of the new school's foundations.

40 We were all invited to throw on more flowers and grains of rice.

41 Some of the children and staff of Shree Sahabir School.

42 The formal exchange of school flags.

43 One of the old school classrooms, small and dark with a mud floor.

44 Handing over our gifts to the school.

45 Namaste!

46 The *mit* ceremony.

villages doesn't start until 10.00 am. On the outskirts of one of the tiny villages we met an old man with a metal artificial leg. He was anxious to be introduced to us as he was an ex-Gurkha who had served with the 6th Gurkha Rifles in World War II. He had fought in Italy which was where he had lost his right foot. He stood to attention, apologising for being in his working clothes, while we took a photograph and promised to try and get it to him somehow. We were to meet quite a few of these old soldiers on our travels, all of whom were very proud to have been in the British army and considered it a great honour to meet an English person. They seem to accept their enforced return to the village life of their childhood with a quiet dignity as it is only those that achieve officer status who are able to improve their standard of living when they return to Nepal.

On the way back to Damauli we had much better views of the Himalayas than we had had on the way up. We saw, for the first time, the full Annapurna range, the Fishtail towering above all of them, which we had only had glimpses of up to now. The highest mountains we had ever seen had been the Alps, but these magnificent peaks made the Alps look like molehills. I shall always remember my first glimpse of the Annapurna range.

"There's the Fishtail over there" said Bill.

"Where, I can't see anything?"

"No, there, look up higher."

I had been staring straight ahead of me, my head tilted at the sort of angle where you might expect to see the tops of mountains in Britain. I realised with a shock how much higher these giants were than anything I had seen previously. They really were in the sky, their snow capped peaks sticking out of the tops of the clouds.

We stopped for what would be our last meal cooked by our tireless porters at a shelter just above the town of Damauli. These porters really were excellent. Not only were we waited on hand and foot but whenever we packed up before setting off, they would carefully check the room where we had slept to make sure we hadn't left anything. Their huge loads were always quickly covered with sheets of plastic at the first sign of any rain and one or other of them was always ready with a helping hand at tricky river crossings. We stopped for lunch at a resting place just above the town of Damauli and here were served with roast potatoes, frankfurters and some delicious apple fritters to follow. We really had been spoiled foodwise but for the rest of our stay in Nepal the standard of food took a downward trend.

It was the end of the school day as we walked across the suspension bridge and through the baking streets of Damauli. Some teenage girls on their way home seemed a little less shy than the girls we had met in the villages and they chatted to us in English. They had come from an all girls school so this probably explained their confidence.

The bus journey back to Pokhara, this time on the faster tourist bus, was a pleasant ride through small towns and villages, all looking much brighter in the sunshine than they had done in the rain of our outward journey. The porters were still with us, ready to help unload the luggage from the roof when we arrived at Pokhara. Everything was a bit rushed, as we loaded our bags into a taxi and the porters sorted out Chandra's gear, so we didn't have time to say goodbye and thank them properly. However, arrangements were made to meet them at Chandra's the next day. The rest of the day was spent doing a bit of sight seeing in Pokhara. We visited a cave which housed a Hindu temple and a god with six heads. Then we went to the famous Devis falls - a thunderous waterfall plunging into a bottomless gorge hundreds of feet below. On a clear day there is a spectacular view of the Annapurna range from Pokhara's other lake, Lake Begnas. However, we were disappointed as the view was obscured by clouds. The lake itself was not as scenic as Phewa Lake and the area was rather uncared for with a lot of litter scattered about. We followed a track round the lake until it gave out after a while and we were held up by two young boys trying to drive their buffaloes back to their village. The buffaloes were quite happy to munch away at the greenery and the boys, who didn't seem in any hurry, were happily throwing sticks up to knock down the clusters of nuts growing in the trees above. These were about the size of a small hazelnut and quite tasty.

Back at Twin Peaks we had a lot of sorting out to do ready for the trek to Annapurna Base Camp. This time we were taking the minimum of gear with us as the weight limit for porters at altitude is thirty kilos. Unfortunately we had somehow missed our appointment at Chandra's with our four porters.

Ramsingh and possibly one of the others were to come with us to Annapurna so at least we would see two of them again. We had run out of all our film and so hadn't taken a photo of them all together so this too, we hoped to do the following day. Gam welcomed us like long lost friends and we enjoyed a welcome shower before I tackled the washing! The next day was supposed to be a rest day before the start of our trek to Annapurna Base Camp. In the morning Chandra came with the forms to fill in for our trekking permits, bringing with him Chitra - one of Dhane's friends-and-relations whom we had already met in Gumlek as his parents lived there. He had returned to Pokhara where he lived with his wife and six year old son. He too was a Gurkha serving in the British army, also on leave and due to return to England at the end of October. He was a bit younger than Dhane - about thirty - and I had got to know him quite well in Gumlek. Here was another example of a father missing his child growing up while he served in Britain for three years at a time, only returning on leave for a maximum of six months. I asked him what had been his impressions of Britain when he first came as a young soldier. He said he had been struck by the cleanliness of the country and fascinated by snow which he had never seen before. This seemed surprising for a person coming from a country of snow covered mountains but the road system is so poor in Nepal that the majority of Nepalis never get anywhere near the mountains. Chandra also introduced to us another Gurkha friend of his who had just retired from the British army. He had been a teacher of Nepali to the British officers. His English was very correct and as he started to explain one or two of the basics of the Nepalese language to me I realised that he must have been an excellent teacher. I'm sure my Nepali would have come on rapidly if I'd had a few lessons with him.

It was after the evening meal that I suffered my first attack of the notorious traveller's diarrhoea which was to recur several times during the rest of our trip. I was never sure as to the cause and can only think that I have a particularly sensitive stomach as we were scrupulous about personal hygiene, ate only cooked food and disinfected all our water with iodine drops. Fortunately we were in the hotel and not too far from the loo but on other occasions on the trek this was not the case. After this first experience I completely lost my appetite - everything I ate seeming to produce the familiar stomach gurglings. However, by sticking to a plain diet and taking Imodium tablets when necessary I managed to cope with the problem. I set our alarm clock for 5.30 the next morning as we were determined once more to try for the promised view from the roof.

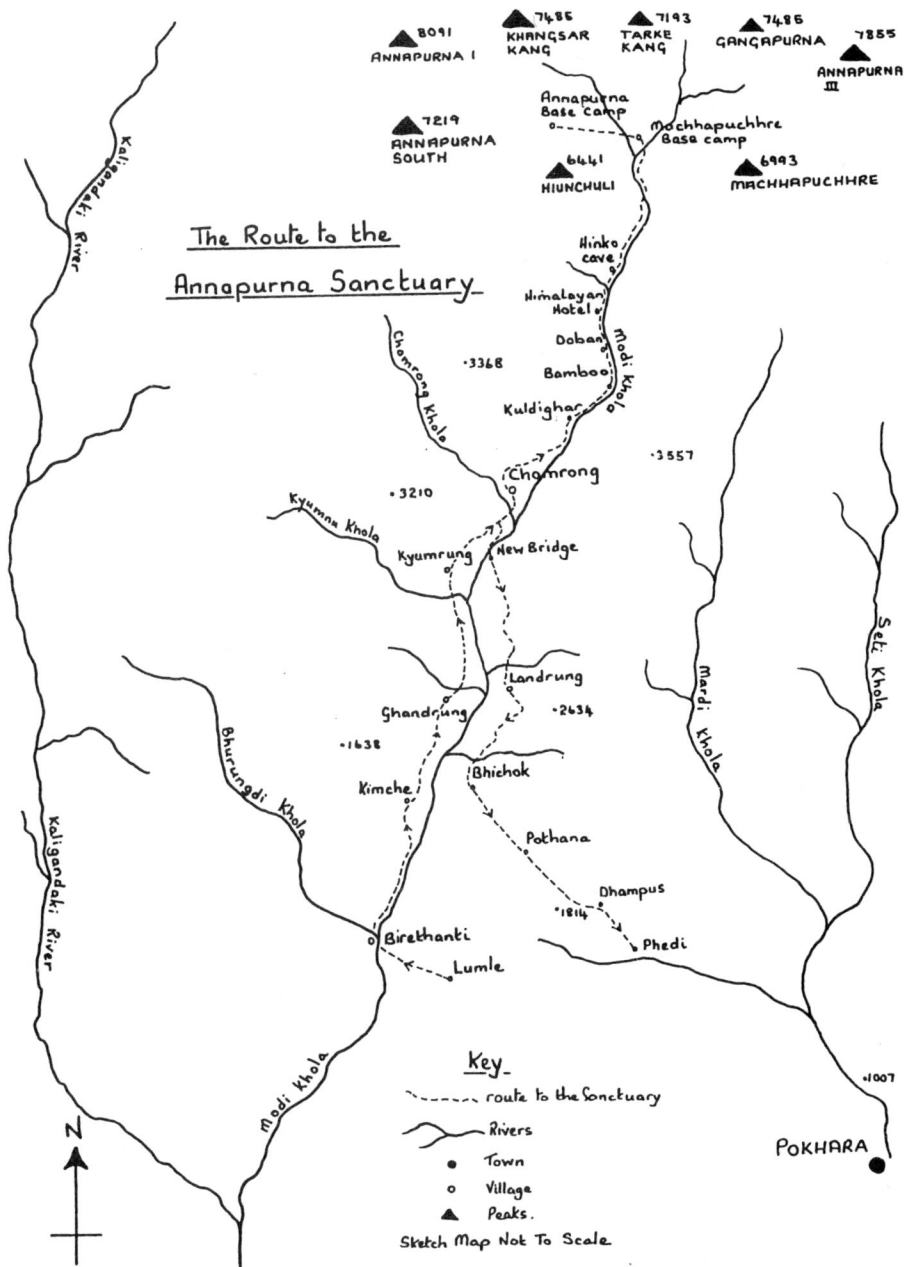

The Route to the Annapurna Sanctuary

Peaks labelled on map:
- 8091 ANNAPURNA I
- 7485 KHANGSAR KANG
- 7193 TARKE KANG
- 7485 GANGAPURNA
- 7855 ANNAPURNA III
- 7219 ANNAPURNA SOUTH
- 6441 HIUNCHULI
- 6993 MACHHAPUCHHRE

Places: Annapurna Base Camp, Machhapuchhre Base Camp, Hinko cave, Himalayan Hotel, Doban, Bamboo, Kuldighar, Chomrong, Kyumrung, New Bridge, Landrung, Ghandrung, Bhichok, Kimche, Pothana, Dhampus, Phedi, Birethanti, Lumle, POKHARA

Rivers: Kaligandaki River, Chomrong Khola, Kyumnu Khola, Bhurungdi Khola, Modi Khola, Mardi Khola, Seti Khola

Spot heights: ·3368, ·3210, ·3557, ·1638, ·2634, ·1814, ·1007

Key
------- route to the Sanctuary
~~~~~ Rivers
● Town
○ Village
▲ Peaks.
Sketch Map Not To Scale

N

69

PART II - THE TREK TO ANNAPURNA BASE CAMP

Chapter 8 - WALL-TO-WALL WATER

I awoke just as the sun was rising after a restless night, due partly to my state of health and partly to my apprehension about the ten-day trek that lay ahead of me. The recommended 'trekking book' time for this particular route varied between two and three weeks. I consider myself only an average walker, having tackled the usual Lake District and Welsh peaks plus a few Scottish munros and a couple of walking holidays in the Alps, so the prospect of being the only female trying to keep up with a young and fit Gurkha soldier was more than a little daunting. However, Dhane had assured me that he would go at our pace and after all I'd had a bit of training on the walk to Gumlek.

All was forgotten, however, when I climbed onto the rooftop to see dawn breaking over the mountains. The whole of the Annapurna range towered above us, bathed in a pinkish light with not a cloud in sight and we clicked away frantically with our cameras. The taxi driver, who had come to take us to Chandra's, said that we were lucky, as this was the first decent view this season. Chandra had our trekking permits ready for us and after a cup of his delicious scented tea we were ready to set off. As we were staying in tea lodges we only needed two porters this time. One of them was dear old Ramsingh and the other was a younger chap called Bhuwan who was training to be a guide and wanted to come to Annapurna Base Camp as he had not been before. Bhuwan was fairly well shod in his own strong looking trainers but Ramsingh had only flip-flops, so our first job was to buy some shoes - ACAP (Annapurna Conservation Area Project) regulations do not permit anyone, porters or otherwise, past the checkpoints unless they are suitably clad as there have been too many deaths, in the past, of porters who have not had enough warm clothes for high altitudes. We eventually fixed Ramsingh up with a pair of 'Goldstar' canvas shoes - I felt he should be wearing boots as we were but was assured that canvas shoes were standard porter's footwear and would pass the ACAP scrutiny. Up to now I had seen very few Nepalis wearing anything other than flip-flops for even the steepest and most slippery of paths. Even Ramsingh did not don his 'Goldstars' until the second day, preferring to tackle the lower slopes in his flip-flops.

The taxi took us to Birethanti which was to be the start of the trek. We were immediately mobbed by young boys

"Nice belts, you buy?"

"You need water? I fetch."

"Bracelet for madam?" (pronounced 'brasslet'.)

"You buy chewing gum?" Dodging the eager faces and outstretched arms we repeated a polite "*Bayo, danyabad*" - Nepali for "Thanks, but no thanks" and started to follow the Modi Khola river through green wooded countryside interspersed with fields of rice, millet and soy bean. I found the plant life in this area especially interesting; there were many species growing wild that are sold as £2.99 house plants in this country, including coleus, hibiscus, and a reddish brown foliage plant which is recommended for bottle gardens. I even saw sensitive plants growing at the side of the path, their leaves folding up obediently when I touched them. In the gardens of the lodges grew more cultivated varieties such as fuchsias, geraniums, bougainvillaea, morning glory and of course the rhododendron which is the national flower of Nepal. This would not be in flower until next March or April. There was also a huge variety of flowers, particularly in the jungle areas, which were native only to Nepal. Some had a lovely scent, others had a sort of curry smell although they were not, in fact, a herb used for curry and tasted revolting. For me the flower that will always remind me of Nepal was tall, bright scarlet and looked similar to an iris but with much broader leaves. These flashy flowers seemed to grow wild as well as in more cultivated areas. I discovered that they grow from a tuber and would have loved to buy some to try out in my greenhouse at home but I'm sure customs would not have allowed them through.

There was an abundance of seasonal fruit at this time - bananas, apples, lemons, limes, oranges (these had green skins but were quite sweet inside) peaches, tomatoes and a cross between a cucumber and a marrow that was very refreshing on a hot day. The most exotic fruit of all, the mango, had been literally dropping off the trees a few weeks earlier but now the trees provided only shade from their huge leaves. We also sampled a small yellow fruit about the size and shape of a lime but with flesh similar in texture and taste to a pear. I think this was a guava, certainly it looked similar to the ones I had seen in Sainsburys. Taking advantage of the glut of fruit were a couple of Nepalis, blocking the path with a huge pile of lemons and an ingenious looking fruit press which consisted of a wooden chute for the juice to run down into a container below and a long pole which was hinged to the chute at the bottom. The lemon was simply squashed in the angle between the chute and the pole by pulling down the end of the pole towards the chute in a sort of scissor movement. Further up we saw more devices such as water wheels, powered by the fast-flowing streams, turning grindstones for maize, all typical of the ever resourceful nature of the Nepalis. At one point a stream had been diverted in such a way as to provide hydro-electric power.

Being a member of the BBCS (British Butterfly Conservation Society), I was also interested in the many species of butterflies. I saw several clouded yellows, various fritillaries, possibly a large tortoiseshell but I wasn't quite sure, blues, orange tips and even the boring old cabbage white. I shall have to identify all the other more exotic ones on my next visit as I didn't manage to buy an identification book until a couple of days before our departure. All the other insects we saw were much larger and more colourful than European varieties. My favourite was a large - about 6 inches long - green creature that looked like a fattish stick insect which, if you could get it to hop over your foot, was supposed to bring good luck.

The villages we were now passing through were obviously more used to tourists than those on the way to Gumlek. Children would run cheekily up to us demanding "One pen" or calling "Hello" and "Bye bye." Instead of the polite exchanges of *Namaste* and stopping to pass the time of day we had become accustomed to on our way to and from Gumlek, we were largely ignored by both villagers and the people we passed on the track. Possibly everyone was too busy to be bothered with us, as all the lodges and hotels along the route had to be kept supplied with food. We saw everything being carried along the path - *dokos* full of bananas, shallower baskets full of tomatoes or green vegetables, even live chickens in wooden cages were carried in the traditional way by means of a band round the forehead. We had to step aside

Steep
slope

Village with
D.I.Y. electric
light.

Black 2"
Hosepipe

small
fan

Small hut
(rabbit hutch size)

*Admiring the do-it-yourself hydro-electric power just south
of Chomrong.*

to let groups of mules laden with potatoes pass by. They looked very much like circus ponies with their brightly coloured harnesses, their red and white horsehair plumes swinging as they tossed their heads.

As regards the native fauna, the most spectacular were the eagles. I had brought binoculars but we didn't need them to view these huge birds which soared only just above our heads, ready to swoop down on an unsuspecting chicken or even a baby goat. We even saw eagles in Kathmandu and Pokhara where they would perch on the rooftops and temples, as common as jackdaws in Britain. Other birds we saw included one or two very brightly coloured birds in the jungle, one with a crest like a cockatoo. The only other creature we actually saw was a rodent which looked just like a rat but that I was assured was only a mouse. We heard deer calling to each other deeper in the jungle and a loud hissing noise which Dhane told us was the sound of a green viper, a highly poisonous snake whose bite can kill within an hour. Coincidentally, only a few days after we returned home I heard on the news that one of these green vipers had escaped from a pet shop causing a bit of a scare until it was found. Dhane had a good snake story, he had been bitten on the arm as a child by a green viper and one of the villagers had put a tourniquet (in the wrong place!) round his wrist and left it until his fingers went numb. Poor Dhane nearly lost the use of his fingers until somebody thought to loosen the tourniquet. He now has two marks on his wrist proving the authenticity of the story! Apart from that, the only other 'wild life' we saw any evidence of was when two women were searching for head lice (or worse!) in each other's hair.

Our first night's stop was at Ghandruk (or Ghandrung, depending on which map you have), a large and important Gurung village with its own particular dialect. Being new to the game of finding the best place to stay, we ignored the tempting signs advertising "Clean beds, good food and wall-to-wall carpet" and we plumped for the highest lodge, where we thought we'd have the best view in the morning if the cloud lifted. It was run by the wife of an ex-Gurkha which, in Dhane's opinion, was a good enough reason for staying there. However, it turned out to be not only one of the worst places we stayed in but also the most expensive. Our room overlooked the backyard where all the rubbish was tipped. The mattresses were damp and the room itself was musty and cell-like with concrete walls and floor. The 'attached bathroom' was a nightmare - the sun had been quite hot earlier in the day so we presumed the solar heating would provide some hot water, and decided to try the shower. This was merely a pipe sticking out from the wall and a small drain hole in the corner of the floor. The shower was OK, nice and warm, but after we'd both showered, we realised that the water wasn't draining away and was in danger of flooding into the bedroom. Subsequent trips to the loo had to be a bare-footed paddle through ankle-deep, and now freezing cold, water! We then discovered that the toilet flush didn't work, and we had to refill the cistern every time we used it by scooping up some of the water from the floor with a rusty kerosene can that we found. To cap it all, the bolt on the door was broken so we had to shove one of the beds against the door to keep it closed at night! When we went down for our meal we were the only people in the dining room. It was served by two giggling fifteen year olds who tried their best to impress both Dhane and Ramsingh, so the evening was spent amusingly enough. However, when we looked down the hill and saw a large party of what looked and sounded like a mixture of nationalities having a great time at the lodge five hundred yards below, we realised that we had made the wrong choice. Grimly we retired to our damp room and wall-to-wall water, resolving to choose more carefully next time.

Chapter 9 - HIGHS AND LOWS

The next morning we learned that Bhuwan would be unable to carry on portering for us as he was having trouble with his ankle. It wasn't too bad at that moment but could get worse if he carried on with a heavy load. Knowing that the cost of porters rises as you go further up towards the Base Camp he decided to quit now while we could still hire another porter at a reasonable price. Bhuwan would still come with us, unpaid and only carrying his own gear, as he was still keen to go to Annapurna Base Camp. Dhane had managed to find a young lad called Ram who, although only seventeen years old assured us he was a porter of some experience and knew the route to ABC, having been several times before. He even came fully shod with his own Wellington boots. The only thing he was short of was a head strap for the rucksack he was to carry, and this we duly purchased before we set off.

Dhane had negotiated a price of two hundred and ten rupees a day, meals not included. Ramsingh was also buying his own meals as Dhane said it was better to offer a higher daily rate and not include meals, because if we were buying the meals the porters could eat as much as they liked at our expense. Porters have huge appetites anyway and if they were buying their own food they would be more economical and would also get their food at 'Nepali price.' Dhane had also bought some extra food in Pokhara before we set off, in the form of bread, snacks, nuts, biscuits and dried noodles which could be either eaten as they were or reconstituted with boiling water. This would help the porters out foodwise as we got higher up because not only does the price of hiring porters increase with altitude but also the price of meals. As with all things, it is a question of supply and demand. There are fewer lodges and tea-houses higher up and less competition so they can charge higher prices. ACAP have controls in this area so that all prices are within certain limits but I believe this is not so in, for example, the Langtang areas. Dhane, shrewd as ever, bought Ram some cigarettes to keep him sweet but then only paid him a daily sum which was just enough to cover his expenses throughout the trek, holding back the balance to give him at the end.

"We do not know him, he might run off with our things if we pay full amount" he explained. This seemed a sound precaution, however, Ram certainly proved himself a good porter, though shy at first he became less so, his face breaking into a huge grin when we teased him about his very deep voice. His load was equal to the size of Ramsingh's and he strode along at twice the speed of everyone else, always first at the resting places and, annoyingly, miles ahead when we wanted anything out of the rucksack, until called back by Dhane.

The inconveniences of the night before were well compensated for. Before we set off, we did get some magnificent views from the roof and, so long as we kept well away from the stink pipe sticking up in the middle, we were able to take some good photos. The path from Ghandruk then followed a series of steep ups and downs as we approached the next largish village of Chomrong. It was during this stretch that Bill realised with horror that the sole of one of his boots was beginning to come away. This is every trekker's nightmare and we didn't even have a back-up pair of trainers. He went very quiet for an hour or so and every time he did speak it was to say something about his boots. We tried to reassure him with phrases like "Nepalis can fix anything" and "You'll have to do it in flip-flops then" but he was not amused. He put his sandals on for a while to try and save the boots for higher up but his ankles started to swell and as the way was slippery and leech-infested this wasn't such a good idea. Just before Chomrong we stopped for lunch and got chatting to a couple of Germans who were travelling through Asia for a whole year! We had had quite a long and tiring morning with all the ups and downs but thought we could get a bit further than Chomrong before stopping for the night. They reassured us that there were plenty of places to stay past Chomrong and also suggested a shop which mainly sold kerosene but might also have some glue for Bill's boots.

The menus at the tea lodges are all the same, the only difference being in the prices which, as I mentioned before, rise as you go higher. Lemon tea, for example, started at five rupees a cup but by the time we got to Machhapuchhare Base Camp it was twenty rupees. Being warned off any sort of dairy produce while I was suffering from diarrhoea I drank quite a lot of lemon tea, it was both refreshing if you were hot and warming if you were cold. Apart from the Nepalese standard food of rice, *dal* and vegetables, various European dishes were on offer such as noodles with vegetables or cheese, fried rice with vegetables, sometimes even pizza or apple pie, a sort of chocolate custard and something called a 'Mars roll' which involved a melted Mars bar with some sort of sauce over it. This sounded pretty revolting anyway and definitely not the sort of thing for a gippy tummy. For those of us on a plain diet there were always eggs, either boiled, fried (or 'fired egg' as we saw on one menu!), poached or an omelette, as well as plain boiled potatoes, (which were full of flavour, being organically grown) chapattis, pancakes and the ubiquitous Tibetan bread.

After lunch we had to deal with the serious problem of the boots and we went in search of some glue. We stopped to ask a woman outside her guest house who was folding sheets - probably to advertise how nice and white they were!

"You stay here, you make me very happy" she coaxed. "I speak good English, you stay here."

When we told her we weren't stopping yet but only wanted to buy some glue she waved her hand in the general direction of a shop which she said was a kerosene store. She was still calling after us as we left.

"You come back, stay here when you come back. Very nice here, very clean."

We found the kerosene store and there, prominently displayed was a card full of tubes of glue. Now I fully intend to write to the manufacturers of this product telling them how wonderful it is, it made all our British glues look like wallpaper paste in comparison. A single application lasted the whole of the rest of the trek, four days of which the boots spent in a permanently wet state due to three days of non-stop rain that swelled the streams we had to cross.

At around dusk we finally stopped at a little place called Sinuwa which was just past the small village of Kuldighar. Sinuwa Lodge was undergoing some alterations, and an extra dining room was being built - a wooden construction rather precariously supported on stilts. Outside there was a complicated arrangement of hosepipes to supply the water tap. When the tap ran dry another pipe was selected and swapped with the existing one until that too ran dry and had to be changed again. We were now quite high up at 2350 metres, certainly this was higher than I had ever been and for the first

Bill getting "stuck in" with the Nepalese glue.

time I dug out my fleece, up to now unused, from the bottom of the rucksack. Our room was quite cosy as, being directly above the kitchen, we had a sort of under floor heating. It even had the windows 'double-glazed' with polythene to keep out the draughts and the corrugated roof was lined with rush matting. We were also given a little candle which cast a warm glow over everything. I have very fond memories of this little lodge and we were to return to it on the way back for a lunch time stop. The owners seem to have gone out of their way to make trekkers welcome and to provide those little extra touches for the comfort of western 'softies'. The food too was of a much better standard than some of the lodges and the owner, sporting a jaunty cowboy hat, was particularly solicitous that everything should be to our liking and kept popping up to the 'dining room' for a bit of a chat with everyone. We decided to break open the two quarter bottles of whisky and rum we had brought with us from Pokhara. These we had bought at a little shop for the amazingly low price of eighty five and sixty five rupees respectively - less than a pound each. The whisky was a bit rough, but drinkable, but the rum was really good, just the job for a chilly evening at altitude, and I vowed to buy some to take home, if only to put in the Christmas cakes.

Most of the other guests were Germans who sat seriously poring over their guide books or scribbling in their diaries while we waited for the meal. We did manage to have a look at one of their guide books which was a lot more informative than our rather inaccurate map which, incidentally, had put Chomrong totally in the wrong place, on the other side of the river, causing some confusion. We could now get a rough idea of the distances, expressed in hours of average walking, between the villages all the way up to Base Camp. We calculated that if we made another of our 'early starts' we could make Machhapuchhare Base Camp before dark the next day.

One of the delicacies offered at Sinuwa Lodge was dried buffalo meat, commonly called buff meat. This is quite chewy with a salty flavour but as I was still sticking to my plain diet and had eaten only soup and plain noodles, I gave my bit to a skinny little kitten which had settled itself on my knee - it too spat it out after a bit. I was just beginning to feel reasonably warm and comfortable, listening to the rain hammering down onto the tin roof when suddenly I felt a familiar churning and had to make a dash for the loo. This

47 The village water tap.

48 The Nepalese are brilliant craftsmen. Here Mum Raj is putting the finishing touches to the *Kainjadi*.

49 Kesh's son with his sculptured statue of a Hindu God.

50 Dhane with his young niece.

51 Posing with some of the mums and their children.

52 Older children are often seen minding younger ones by carrying them on their backs.

53 Bill and I with Kesh Bahadur and his wife at their village of Bhirkot.

54 The Bhirkot 'mother's union' or Ama Party.

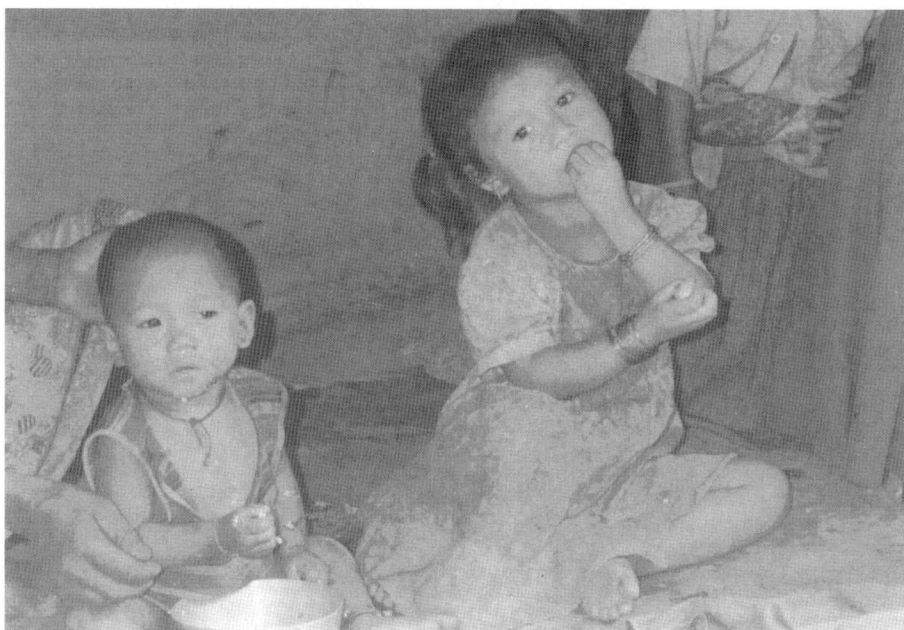

55 Village children enjoying their rice.

56 A typical village house.

57 Chatting to some of the girls from a school in Damauli.

involved climbing over the bench seat, squeezing past the still seated party of Germans, wrestling with the sliding door then nearly falling down the rickety steps outside before groping my way through the darkness to the opposite end of the building where, as luck would have it, the one and only loo was occupied. Just as I was beginning to think I'd have to dive into some nearby bushes, the occupant emerged. I was to spend the rest of the evening getting to know this small concrete cubicle quite well, but finally after five or six more trips I crawled, totally exhausted, into my sleeping bag. I had hit an all time low. Just as I had begun to think the problem had gone away, it was back again with a vengeance. I hardly dared go to sleep, but knew I had to get some rest if I was to make tomorrow's target of Machhapuchhare Base Camp. Fortunately the Imodium tablets again did the trick and I was able to snatch a few hours sleep before 'reveille' at 6 am. It could be worse, I consoled myself, at least I didn't have dysentery. We had met an Australian and his wife earlier in the day in deep consultation with a German gentleman who had a suitcase full of all sorts of medicaments. We got talking to him later and, being fairly ignorant about such things and wanting to reassure myself, I had asked him how you know it's dysentery and not just ordinary traveller's diarrhoea.

"Well, with dysentery you start losing bits of your insides" he explained "But I'll be OK, I've still got about twenty percent of my body fat left and I can hold water down for twenty minutes now." - this last statement pronounced as if it were a real achievement! He looked dreadful and so did his wife who, herself, was just recovering from being ill for a week. In the face of such optimism my problems paled into insignificance. However, we never saw him again, so whether he had had to give up and seek proper medical assistance further down, or had been able to rest up and recover sufficiently to continue, we never found out. If his determination was anything to go by he would have made it somehow.

Chapter 10 - *PANI PARYO*

I awoke in the morning with a raging thirst and after a breakfast of Dioralyte mixed with water, I carefully made up three litres of iodine treated water and added a well know brand of energy-giving powder that sportsmen use, to sustain me through what was to be the most strenuous day so far, as by now I had completely lost my appetite.

We were now about to enter the most spectacular part of the trek through the deep Modi Khola gorge. It was a dismal morning and although not actually raining, the mist was down so we couldn't see a thing. The first part took us through a bamboo jungle where, after about an hour, we came to the ACAP checkpoint. All trekkers have to register in a book and state their destination and must do the same on the way back so that if anyone did go missing this information would be some sort of rough guide as to the time and place of their disappearance. However, since there are no telephones or radios up here, the only means of contacting the checkpoint would be by a messenger on foot which would not lead to a very speedy search-and-rescue operation. About half an hour further on we reached the appropriately named Bamboo and stopped for breakfast. These stopping places, in fact all the stopping places after Chomrong, were no longer villages at all but merely groups of lodges built solely for the use of trekkers. By now a steady drizzle was falling and we were happy to shelter for a while. I managed to force down half a chapatti and a cup of lemon tea and we set off again, not really gaining much height now as we walked through the dripping jungle.

Suddenly, out of the gloom we saw a tall figure with a ski pole in each hand and both knees strapped up, but still managing to keep up quite a speed, come charging towards us. We didn't think much about it at the time but we discovered later that this was actually Joe Simpson a writer of many mountaineering books, the most famous of which was called 'Touching the Void' which Bill had only just finished reading, telling an incredible story of how he had fallen down a crevasse in Peru and managed to survive against all odds.

The Modi Khola was far below us but we couldn't see it until we emerged from the jungle. Here were the spectacular cliffs and plunging waterfalls that we had read about in this part of the gorge. Had the day been clear we would also have had magnificent views of the Fishtail and Annapurna but even so the gorge was pretty awesome. The massive cliffs towered above us and waterfalls hundreds of feet high seemed to cascade from the sky.

I, however, was feeling pretty weak by now and it was all I could do to keep putting one foot in front of the other. Dear Ramsingh kept me company at the back and we kept our spirits up by conversing in a sort of pidgin Nepali/English. In this area were some deliciously scented flowers.

"*Phul?*" I asked pointing to one.

"*Phul*" affirmed Ramsingh with a more correct pronunciation.

"*Malai, phul ramro.*" (I like flowers). We continued in this vein, he correcting my pronunciation of such words as *oraalo* (downhill), *ukaalo* (uphill), *bistare* (slowly), *biraami* (sick), *pani paryo* (it's raining), *pani parena* (it's stopped raining) and other such phrases.

"Modi Khola?" I asked, pointing to the river.

"Coca cola, mem Sahib?" replied Ramsingh with a puzzled look.

"No Modi Khola."

"Ah! Modi Khola! Modi Khola, Coca-cola, Modi Khola, Coca-cola!" This then became a catchphrase, of course, repeated ad nauseum in the same way as people do daft things when they are tired or recovering from an illness in a hospital ward and the slightest thing seems to set everyone off into giggles.

We stopped at the famous Himalaya Hotel for lunch; this stopping place had a couple of well-built lodges with slate roofs and a camping area. After half a bowl of soup we trudged on, the trail now getting narrower as it climbed up, sometimes opening up to get a misty view of the towering cliffs above. By now Ramsingh was carrying my daysac as well as his main load, otherwise I would have lagged behind even further. The temperature was now beginning to drop and the rain was a steady downpour. In fact if you closed your eyes you could well imagine yourself on a typical English Lake District walk!

It was a good thing we hadn't decided to stop at Hinko cave - a huge overhanging cliff where there had once been a lodge. It had been reduced to rubble by a recent landslide and there was only the cave left intact which would provide some sort of shelter in an emergency. We were now at about 3,000 metres and everyone was slowing down a bit due to the altitude. I had heard so much about altitude and how it affects different people that I was quite disappointed to find that I didn't even get a headache. I was totally exhausted anyway, and I didn't know whether this was due to lack of food, the altitude or a combination of both. After what seemed like hours of doggedly putting one foot in front of the other, concentrating all the time so as not to slide off the now treacherously slippery path, a long low building came into sight.

"This is it!" shouted Bill. "Thank God for that" I thought as I summoned my last ounce of strength. Dhane went on ahead as it was by now getting close to 5 o'clock and the few lodges at Machhapuchhare Base Camp would quickly fill up. The Fishtail Lodge that we were heading for was actually quite a few hundred yards further on than the low building we had seen and was, as we had feared, full. However, we managed to get rooms in one of the other three lodges. Absolutely soaked to the skin, we lashed out fifty rupees on a bowl of luke-warm water, had a quick wash in the concrete cubicle proudly calling itself a bathroom and then joined the rest of the guests at the lodge in the large dining room. A huge table took up most of the room, round the edge of which were either benches or wider platforms where the dark heads of porters could be seen sticking out from under blankets and duvets as they slept or simply kept warm. Underneath the table the floor was sunken and in the middle was a powerful kerosene heater. The whole of the sunken floor area was covered in wet clothing and in addition there was a string 'washing line' all round the edge of the table where you could hang smaller items to dry. Outside the string but also fixed around the edge of the table and reaching the floor level were blankets and these served not only to keep the heat in under the table and so dry everything off quicker, but also to stop one burning one's knees, as the heat from the heater was really quite intense.

I must have sat for an hour or two in a trance, enjoying the warmth and the fact that I had actually made it and didn't have to plod on any further - at least not until tomorrow. As I gradually recovered I became aware of a group of three Australians who must have formed the ideal walking group. One, Liz, was a nurse with a bag full of tablets and medicaments which she was distributing to anyone who needed anything, another, Kath, was a physiotherapist and the third, James, was a sports scientist. Bill had by now developed quite a bad headache and, having experienced altitude before in the Alps, knew this to be an altitude headache. Liz sorted him out with some Dimox tablets, so then I moved round the table to have a chat with her about my own problem. Having listened to my symptoms and reassured me that she didn't think it was anything serious requiring antibiotics she then advised me.

"Ya gotta eat, ya gotta keep shovin it down - all plain stuff, no sugar, just plain boiled rice and potatoes. Here, have some of these, they're delicious. Ya gotta eat plenty of carbohydrate 'cos ya can't get yer energy from sweet stuff 'cos that's no good for the diarrhoea."

"Yeah, ya gotta eat else ya'll hit the wall" joined in James.

"Hit the wall?"

"Yeah, I hit the wall once, just stopped, collapsed, couldn't go no further; I'd used up all my body reserves. Didn't git no warning, just all of a sudden - bang! wallop! I'd hit the wall!"

Determined not to 'hit the wall' myself, I ordered a plate of plain boiled rice. Bill had ordered a huge meal but by the time it came he'd lost his appetite, another common symptom of high altitude, so most of that got passed round the table.

By now all the wet clothes were gently steaming, a card game was in full swing, and diaries were being scribbled while the lodge cooks were busily slaving away next door in the kitchen. These kitchens really are amazing places - on a couple of kerosene stoves they can produce anything from apple pie to pizza! There is always a huge panful of rice on the go and a pressure cooker, containing the vital *dal*, hissing away. All this is done in complete darkness, the one Tilley lamp being reserved for the dining area. Everyone was reluctant to leave the warmth of this room as the bedrooms were particularly cold and damp because of the continuous rain. We talked about the possibility of a view from Annapurna Base Camp which, although only two and a half kilometres further up, was about a two hour walk at this altitude,

ABC being just over 4,000 metres. However, this rain was set to stay for the next day or two so we would have to sit it out here for another two days for any hope of a view. We were on a fairly tight schedule and had to be back in Pokhara in four days so we just didn't have the time. If, by some miracle, the weather cleared overnight, the best plan would be to set off at about 3 am to arrive at ABC just as dawn was breaking, but in the circumstances this looked unlikely.

Just as I was thinking about leaving the warmth and conviviality to catch up on some well-earned sleep, James, one of the Australian medical team, stood up and said to Kath (the physiotherapist).

"OK Kath, are you just gonna take a look at my knees before I hit the sack?" I pricked up my ears at the mention of the word 'knees' as I have suffered a fair amount of pain from my knees when descending steep slopes and wasn't much looking forward to the start of the descent for this very reason.

"Do you know about knees then?" I asked.

"Oh yeah, she's an expert. Just been on a course. What she don't know about knees ain't worth knowin'. You tell her, Kath."

I couldn't believe my luck, Kath had just been on a course on knee injuries and had learnt about a new technique - I think it was called the McGregor technique - actually from the person who had invented it. It involved sticking strips of that old-fashioned zinc oxide sticking plaster, the non-stretchy sort, across the kneecap. Six or seven strips about six inches long are stuck overlapping each other and the idea is to support the kneecap. The strips are placed either slightly above or slightly below the kneecap, according to where the pain is felt. Anyway, after she'd done James's knees - he'd had a serious injury resulting in damage to his kneecap, whereas my problem was just general wear and tear to the cartilage - I got Kath to have a look at mine. Obviously she couldn't make a full assessment without a proper examination but she stuck me some strips of plaster on. These were really tight and presented a bit of a problem when squatting down to use the loo. However, I was to be amazed at the efficacy of this treatment and the sticking plaster stayed in place, if working a bit loose, for the next four days.

That night the temperature dropped to about freezing and I was glad that I had decided to bring my rather bulky three season sleeping bag. We had not really gone in for much lightweight gear as yet and my bag was of the bung-it-in-the-car variety. Every morning I wrestled with a compression spider to try to get it as small as possible but that didn't make any difference to the weight so I was pleased I didn't have to carry it.

I had just drifted rather damply off to sleep when I was suddenly woken by screams coming from the next room. Lights were seen to flash through the cracks in the wooden partition.

"It's a rat! Hey, get that thing outta here!"

"Aw shut up, it can't be, ya can't get rats at this altitude!"

"I tell ya, it's a rat, it's too big for a mouse! Get that stick!" Sounds of a chase ensued, doors banged, sticks whacked down. The rat had obviously been scared witless by these noisy foreigners and had gone to ground somewhere. Eventually peace resumed.

Just as it was starting to get light somebody's alarm trilled further down the building. Bill peered out of the window and reported that the mist was still down and it was chucking it down with rain so there wasn't any point in rushing up to Annapurna Base Camp. Only slightly disappointed, I stuck my head back inside my hood and tried for another hour or two's sleep. It was only when the sound of other people stirring woke me later on that the full impact of the state of affairs hit me. It was still raining hard and we could see that there had been a snowfall overnight as the near, lower peaks were dusted with white. However, everything else was shrouded in mist, and there was nothing to indicate that there would be any change in the next few hours, or even days. Slowly a sense of hopeless disappointment descended on us. We clutched at straws - perhaps it would lift by lunchtime? Maybe by some miracle it would be clear at Annapurna Base camp? However, we all knew that there was no point in wasting valuable energy going on up when there was absolutely no chance of a view for at least twenty-four hours. I felt a bit better after a night's sleep and would have liked to carry on just to be able to say we'd been there but I was afraid that I would slow everybody down on the way back. I am particularly slow going downhill anyway and I didn't know, at this moment in time, how my knees were going to be. The consensus of opinion was that we should head back down. We took a few daft, dismal photos of ourselves standing under our umbrellas in the rain trying to get the snowy bits in the background, then slowly we resigned ourselves to bitter disappointment. To have come all this way to see, not the awe-inspiring panorama of some of the world's highest mountains we had dreamed about, but to be surrounded by mist and rain was, to say the least, heart-breaking. We hung about and slowly packed our things hoping against hope that there would be a break in the cloud or just the slightest excuse for us to carry on up but there was no change. Bhuwan had nipped up on his own, wanting to check out the route and we spent the first part of the descent regretting that we hadn't gone with him but there was no way I could have kept up his pace - he was up and back in an hour and a half - and so this would have delayed us quite considerably.

Our regrets and disappointments were soon pushed aside, however, as the first part of the descent proved even more treacherous than the ascent the day before. Paths were now slippery streams and streams had swollen to raging torrents. In several places the flimsy log bridges had been washed away or looked decidedly unsafe so we had to cross by forming a chain and wading through. The porters did their best by throwing in extra stones at strategic places but avoiding being soaked up to the knees was impossible. Amazingly, the glue on Bill's boots seemed to be holding out remarkably well against all this water.

Lunch was at the Himalaya Hotel again but this time we stayed inside. It was much cooler and the rain was relentless. Poor Ram was shivering, being quite inadequately clothed in just a T-shirt with a cotton shirt on top but we just didn't have any spare dry clothing to give him. I was trying to save my one pair of dry socks to change into in the evenings and James, one of the Australians, had joked that morning. "I should keep quiet about that, there are people here who would kill for a pair of dry socks!" I had been debating whether it was better to put on wet socks or to use my last pair of dry ones but had come to the conclusion that, since they would get wet anyway within ten minutes, I might as well put on the wet ones and look forward to dry ones at the end of the day. I can now understand mountaineers on expeditions arguing over the last square of chocolate, as these minute creature comforts tend to assume much greater magnitude when they are in such short supply.

If you ever go to Nepal I do recommend you to try their potatoes. The taste is a far cry from the typical bland, fluffy taste of an English spud. These were full of flavour and I can only assume that this is partly due to their small size and partly the fact that they are completely organically grown. When I say organic, not only is animal waste used to fertilize the soil but, having no flush toilets in most areas, the Nepalis throw all their human waste on the fields as well. The potatoes are boiled in the pan, skins, mud and all and so as long as you are careful when peeling them, they make a delicious change from rice.

I was feeling fighting fit by now and was really enjoying the experience of negotiating the swollen streams and rivers. We stopped at about 4.00 pm however, as the track had been quite busy and lodges would soon be filling up. As it was, we were lucky to get in at Dovan - Annapurna Approach Lodge - and took the last two rooms.

That night was a truly international gathering comprising two New Zealanders, two French guys, some Germans, two Americans and an Israeli plus ourselves and the Nepalis. One of the Americans was an aid worker who had been working for CARE in Bangladesh, on a road-building project. Fero, an Israeli travelling on his own, arrived at the lodge about an hour after dark, soaking wet but raving on about some snow at Annapurna Base Camp - he hadn't seen snow before. He hadn't seen much else as the mist had been right down but there had been snow on the ground. All rooms were taken by now but Dhane agreed to share as there was a spare bed in his room. Upon further enquiry I learnt that they always manage to pack everybody in somehow, even if it is just a mat on the balcony. We were only at the beginning of the season so things were relatively quiet. In the height of the season the three or four lodges would not be enough to provide rooms for everyone. Back at Twin Peaks we were to meet an Austrian who had just completed the Annapurna circuit. He had not even taken a sleeping bag, and had relied on the lodges and their blankets all the way and had never been turned away, something that probably would not have been possible later on in the season.

The rest of the evening was spent playing Fero's word game. I think he takes this game wherever he goes; he was a fascinating and tremendously well educated man who spoke excellent English and was hoping to come to the UK to do a degree in Psychology at Edinburgh University. This word game was really an opportunity for him to astonish everybody with his general knowledge and his command of the English language, but it passed the evening amusingly enough, while we listened to the rain hammering on the tin roof and dried our clothes on a similar washing line arrangement to the night before. This time, when we got the bill in the morning we found we had been charged thirty rupees for the heater! Still it was well worth it.

In the morning there were a couple of patches of blue but the mist soon came down again. Glancing up at the lodge next door while cleaning my teeth I heard familiar voices.

"Would ya believe it? It's still raining!"

It was Kath and Liz, the Australians. They too must have given up on ABC and followed us down. I went in to congratulate Kath on the success of her knee tapes.

"I'll just stick you a couple more on and that should see you okay back to Pokhara."

There is nothing like putting your faith in something to give you encouragement. By now I really was beginning to believe in this technique, so whether it was 'all in the mind' or whether it was really working was immaterial; it gave me the confidence to take on the downhill stretches with gusto, knowing that I would be without the usual excruciating pain in my knees.

The weather was unrelenting; everyone we passed going up sympathised but they knew that they were in with a better chance so they could afford to be magnanimous. We stopped for lunch at our favourite spot - Sinuwa Lodge. I was suddenly brought to my senses while talking to a young American girl less than half my age who said they were taking eleven days to do the ABC trek and that was just up! We had been trekking for only five days and had been up and halfway down again. This realisation had the double effect of making me feel quite pleased with myself that I'd made the distance in less than half the time of this much younger person; and also of making me think what a pity it was that we'd only got seven days for the trek and how much better it would have been to have been able to take it at a more leisurely pace. I was now even more determined to come back and do the trek again, allowing much more time.

After lunch it stopped raining briefly and I got talking to a group of about six Australian women of a similar age to myself. Inevitably the subject turned to aches and pains and of course - knees. I began singing the praises of Kath's revolutionary tape treatment and rather foolishly mentioned that she was only just behind us. Immediately all six determined that they would tackle Kath with their own various knee problems. Whether they found her and if they did whether the roll of sticky tape lasted out, I will never know - I can only hope that, as a fellow Australian, Kath was sympathetic to their demands!

It became obvious, as we carried on down towards Chomrong, that most people were just setting off. We were now a week into October and as the best views are supposed to be seen from the middle to the end of October, we had been just that little bit too early. We passed numerous Brits and wished them luck and better views than we had had. They, in turn warned us of heavy leeches ahead; this however, was now a minor problem compared to everything else we had encountered. The leeches seemed to like Ramsingh though, and he ended up with about six sticking plasters on each foot by the evening.

I had forgotten about the long descent from Chomrong, made only slightly easier by the steps. This of course, was now reversed and we had about 2,000 steps to climb to reach Chomrong. About halfway up we heard "Hi, you guys!" and who should we see, roaring up the steps behind us, but James, from the Australian party.

"The girls have sent me on ahead to find somewhere to stay, they're just about all in" he explained.

Remembering the persuasive lady with the beautiful white sheets from on the way up, we directed him to her hotel, assuring him with broad winks and nudges that she would 'make him very happy.'

The sun was now beginning to peep through and we could actually see some of the peaks when the clouds parted. It had been so long since we'd seen anything but mist that we stopped for a drink at Chomrong. We sat on the balcony of a pretty little lodge whose kitchen equipment, neatly arranged for all to see, glinted in the sunlight and we felt we were getting back into civilisation as women came to the nearby tap to fill their water pots and wash their clothes and children came to have a look at us. It would have been pleasant to linger in this village but our destination for the night was a place called Hot Springs where there was actually a hot spring and a giant concrete tub where the water was about one hundred degrees fahrenheit. This was a different route to the one we had taken on the way up, as we planned to return along the other side of the valley via Landruk and the Dhampus area. When we arrived at Hot Springs the following sign greeted us:

DEAR TREKERS
HOTSPRING OPENING NOW
(DO NOT USE SOAP IN HOTSPRING BATH)
HOTSPRING IS 15 MINUT
NO GUEST HOUSE AND RESTAURANT IN
HOTSPRING SO THAT IF YOU BUY SOMETHING
POSSIBLE HEAR
                                    THANKS

We saw many such notices along the way, all charmingly misspelt and sometimes rather ambiguous in meaning. The actual hot spring turned out to be a good hour's walk from the lodge. Since it would be improper for me to strip off and plunge into the 'bath' as I would dearly have loved to do, Dhane and the porters went down while Bill and I bought a bucket of hot water for thirty rupees and had a pleasant enough wash in a shed behind the hotel with beautiful jungle views and birds hopping about outside. Dhane returned about one and a half hours later complaining that the wash at Hot Springs had been a waste of time as he'd got all sweaty again coming back up the hill - "serves him right for walking too fast", I thought. The sun had cheered us all up and we hung our clothes on the balcony and finished off the rest of the rum to celebrate. After the evening meal Bill had a sudden urge for a Mars bar.

We had tried a Snickers bar bought in Pokhara and it tasted really awful. We couldn't decide whether this was a mouldy taste because it was well past its death date (as much of the chocolate is in Nepal) or whether, being made in Turkey or somewhere, it was supposed to taste like that. Anyway, the Mars bar was pronounced delicious, just the same as English ones. I wasn't quite ready for Mars bars yet but I did try a little *dal* with my rice.

Chapter 11 - THE LAST LEG

The next morning dawned bright, sunny and cloud-free. Eager to make up for the lack of views the day before and as it was fairly early, only 6.30 am, we decided to walk back up the hill for half an hour or so to get a good view of the Fishtail before the clouds covered it. Our efforts were rewarded and we were just in time to get a superb view of the fish's tail part of the mountain before it finally went behind the clouds ten minutes or so later. There was a handy little cafe where we enjoyed a cup of tea in the early morning sunshine. The owner, who was a shoemaker and smelt a little too strongly of *raksi* for this hour, asked us if we would take a photo of him and post it to him. This we did, promising that we'd try and get the photo to him this time as many people had taken photos before and had not bothered to send him a copy.

After a while we headed back down to the lodge. This particular lodge, called the Namaste Hotel, was advertising toast on its menu. After a diet of boiled eggs and chapattis this really was a luxury. Nepali bread is slightly sweet and the buttered toast and eggs we had for breakfast were delicious. That morning we had a pleasant, if somewhat leech infested, walk along the other side of the Modi Khola river; lunch and a leech check were spent at Landruk, a small village just about opposite Gandrung on the other side of the river. Ramsingsh's 'Goldstars' were now coming adrift after all the rain so we spread them out to dry and then got to work with the Nepalese glue. On the way out of the village we passed the village school where there seemed to be a very rough game of tig going on. One little boy managed to get quite a nasty cut on his face and retreated, crying, behind a wall. We tried to get him to accept a plaster to stick on the wound but to no avail. Such incidents appear to be commonplace in the schools where there is no supervision of play and no compulsion even to come to school.

The afternoon took us through more villages - a steepish climb first and then a pleasant walk along a path which had stones laid in a sort of crazy-paving style for a good part of the way. Tall trees either side made us almost feel as though we were walking through the grounds of a stately home! The views were getting better and better as we descended, but unfortunately we had run out of all our film except for black and white. Finally we arrived at Potana, a very busy, touristy village which was full of various trekking parties. As we walked through the village we passed three English girls dressed only in swimming costumes, washing themselves at the village tap.

"Do you not respect these people's religion? You should be ashamed of yourselves! You are insulting their people with your behaviour!"

This was a German gentleman admonishing the girls in a loud voice for their indiscretion. None of the Nepalis were actually taking much notice and the girls said that they had asked permission, but then what Nepali in his right mind is going to refuse a free peep show?

Tonight's lodge was romantically named Heavens Gate which I suppose it was, compared to some of the places we had stayed at. We had a rush mat to cover the mud floor, a lukewarm shower and electricity for two hours during the evening! That night was to be the last with the porters, although Bhuwan had already left us at Chomrong to go off on his own, so we bought some bottles of beer which was quite expensive at one hundred rupees a bottle, and some *raksi* for Ram.

Most of the inside dining room was taken up with a noisy party of French who filled the room with their loud chatter and Gauloise cigarette smoke. We had met this party on the way up and I, eager to show off my French to compensate for the fact that I couldn't speak much Nepali, had spoken to them about their trip. They were being taken round various 'villages typiques' in the area, or so they had been told. I hadn't liked to disillusion them as really the villages in this popular trekking area were not at all typical of Nepalese villages. I realised how privileged we were to have our own link with a genuinely typical Nepalese village together with all the unique opportunities it offered for mutually benefitting our two so very different cultures.

Ram had drifted off to join a card game to see if he could lose the rest of his porter's pay before the final pay-off the next day. Meanwhile we began chatting to three girls from Singapore whose table we were hoping to use when they had finished their meal; the lodge was so crowded that table space was in very short supply. We decided, as it was our last night, to try the famous 'apple pie' that had featured on many of the tea house menus. I wondered, in my conventional way, where they would roll out the pastry and how they would cook it without an oven but when it came it was a sort of apple puree sandwiched between two thick pancakes which must have been fried in the same pan that was used for pancakes, pizzas, omelettes and everything else. Although a far cry from the traditional English version it was fairly palatable.

I was going to miss Ramsingh and Ram whom we had got to know so well. Ram with his deep voice and beaming smile, echoing our whistling and mimicking our English, and Ramsingh, solicitous to a fault but equally ready for a laugh and a joke. As Ramsingh was one of the Pahar Trust's regular cook/porters, we would probably see him again on future visits, and we sat in the darkness, amicably planning future trips. We assured Ramsing that we could manage quite well without the wooden toilet seat and that next time we'd bring our own lightweight tent and other lightweight gear. I resolved to try and think of a suitable present for him to remind him of the trek.

The next day dawned fine and clear and Bill rushed off to find a viewpoint to take some final pictures of what was really one of the best mountain views so far. During breakfast, which was delicious toasted bread cakes, Ramsingh managed to get hold of a bundle of about fifty friendship bands. These, I was sure, would sell well back in England and raise money for the fund. They were beautifully made, the patterns much more intricate and colourful than any I had seen in England and Ramsingh had negotiated a good price.

It was a mere two or three hours walk from Potana back through the now familiar rice fields and the villages of the Dhampus area to the roadside. We had been warned that this area was 'bandit country' and certainly there were plenty of young boys hovering as we passed through the various villages; they rushed up to us, asking for 'one pen'. On one occasion Bill stopped to put a film in his camera and three or four boys came up and started pulling at his rucksack, trying to undo it, and he had to physically push them off. The eyes of even the youngest children seemed to be everywhere as they hung about, looking for the main chance.

"You must look angry, not smile" Dhane advised "You don't put anything down, they take, then they run like hell!"

58 The Kali Gandaki, Nepal's sacred river, viewed from Bhirkot.

59 Looking up the Modi Khola gorge with the sacred Machhapuchhare (the fishtail) on the right in cloud.

60 The lemon squeezer!

61 Looking for head-lice!

62 Mules carrying supplies.

63 Villagers sawing planks in the traditional way.

64 Carrying fruit and vegetables to supply the tea houses.

65 En route for Annapurna Base Camp.

66 Terraced fields of rice, as we headed up the Modi Khola towards Gandruk.
67 Inside a typical tea house.

68 Crossing one of the many precarious bridges up the Modi Khola.

69 Looking down the Modi Khola gorge from Machhapuchhare Base Camp.

Much sooner than we expected, we reached the roadside and sat down while Bill and Dhane sorted out Ram's pay. We were serenaded by two Nepalis playing Nepalese violins - *saringhi*. These are only about a foot long and played with a bow but with the instrument resting on the knee. The neck and body are intricately carved with various designs or pictures of the gods. We paid Ram, together with a generous tip, entreating him not to spend it all on cards and cigarettes and he beamed at us as he waved goodbye and set off, wellies squelching, back to his village of Ghandruk. Ramsingh returned to Pokhara with us in the taxi, dropping his rucksack off at his house on the way. He spends the trekking season in Pokhara but returns with his family for the winter to his village high up in the jungle. Determined not to miss saying goodbye to him this time we arranged to meet at Twin Peaks the next day.

The sun was beating down in Pokhara so we spread all our wet gear out to dry in the glorious sunshine. Everything was muddy but I was determined only to wash the essentials. Gam greeted us with the sad news that while we had been away Chandra's father had unfortunately died. He was ninety-four and had been ailing for some time. This meant that Chandra, being a Buddhist, was officially in mourning for fourteen days. We went to visit him later in the afternoon and had a fascinating insight into the Buddhist funeral arrangements. Chandra himself had had his head shaved and was only allowed to eat one meal a day for thirteen days and this should contain no meat. He was not allowed to laugh or indulge in any light-hearted activities, so the plan to take us to a popular nightspot in Pokhara called Open House was understandably abandoned. One of the rooms of his house was turned into a Buddhist temple with replicas of Buddha and various gods and other accoutrements pertaining to the Buddhist religion. Every day for seven days a priest would come to this room and stay all day reading the Buddhist 'bible' from start to finish, while outside the room one hundred and eight candles were kept burning representing the fifty-four warriors and the fifty-four peace lovers. Neighbours, friends and relatives would visit each day to pay their respects before the cremation at the end of the fourteen days. We were offered fruit, as presumably was everyone else who visited. An in-depth study of Buddhism would be required to understand the many and complicated rites but the visit certainly left me with the feeling that Chandra's father had been both dearly loved and respected by everyone who knew him and that the various rituals and ceremonies gave everyone a chance to honour this highly respected person in a way that few English funerals can.

Earlier in the afternoon we had experienced the Nepalese black market. Completely spent up after the trek we needed to change some travellers cheques in order to pay both Chandra and the hotel bill. We set off towards the main part of Pokhara in search of a bank. However, we were sidetracked on the way by a book shop and, thinking they might also sell camera film, we went in. After a few minutes browsing, during which we managed to collect quite a pile of books and maps, we realised we couldn't pay for any of it without first getting some rupees from somewhere. We asked the shop owner where the nearest bank was.

"I give you good rate, better than bank" was his reply and as we needed to change quite a large amount of money we negotiated a rate of 89.5 rupees to the pound sterling which was considerably better than the bank's 87.5 and without their one percent surcharge. He made a couple of phone calls and I duly countersigned three hundred and fifty pounds worth of travellers cheques, entrusted them to the shopkeeper who then zoomed off on his motorbike. We waited rather anxiously in the shop, but ten minutes later he re-appeared with our rupees, so all was well. Quite what was in it for him I wasn't sure but there can be no doubt that there was some profit for him somewhere. We got a pretty good discount on the books and maps too, and left the shop feeling quite pleased with ourselves.

Our next visit was to honour our promises to purchase our gifts from the persuasive ladies at the Tibetan village and when we finally managed to get away we set off to look for a present for Ramsingh. Eventually we decided on a purple waterproof with a hood which was big enough at the back to cover his rucksack. This seemed about the most appropriate gift and would remind him of our rainy trip to Annapurna.

The next day was supposed to be a rest day spent sight-seeing and shopping in Pokhara but as we had already done quite a bit of both we decided to head for Kathmandu a day early. Dhane must surely be anxious to rejoin his wife and children having already spent nearly two weeks of his precious leave away from them, so we nipped back to the hotel to bring our washing in before dark and then called a taxi to take us to Chandra's. Chitra, a Gurkha soldier and one of Dhane's friends-and-relations whom we had met in Gumlek had invited us to his house on the outskirts of Pokhara, so after we left Chandra we directed the taxi to Chitra's house. I was slightly concerned about the taxi meter which had already been ticking away for about an hour while we had been at Chandra's. We now clocked up another hour's worth while we had a cup of tea with Chitra and his wife and young son. I had grown used to the idea, by now, that I would not see much of Chitra's wife; she brought the tea and then disappeared back into the kitchen again, re-appearing only to say goodbye when we left. Chitra was due back in England in mid-October and we invited him to come with Dhane to stay with us. Here was another example of a young family split in two for the next three years until Chitra's next leave.

It was getting late and we still had a mountain of packing to do if we were to be ready for the bus which left at 10.30 the next morning. We had purchased three bus tickets, two tourist and one Nepali price, earlier in the day so we were now committed to this famous bus trip from Pokhara to Kathmandu. I was not looking forward to this journey, having heard too many tales of buses going over the edge of the hairpin bends on the approach to Kathmandu, but I pushed such thoughts and fears to the back of my mind. I needn't have worried about the taxi because, although we had used some three or four hours of his time, the bill only came to four hundred rupees - a very modest sum by English standards.

The rest of the evening was spent trying to pack all our gear, some of which was still wet, due to a late afternoon shower. I'm afraid that the exertions of the past seven days were now beginning to tell and I collapsed into bed, leaving Bill to do most of the packing.

"I'll be okay in the morning" were my last words as I fell into an exhausted sleep.

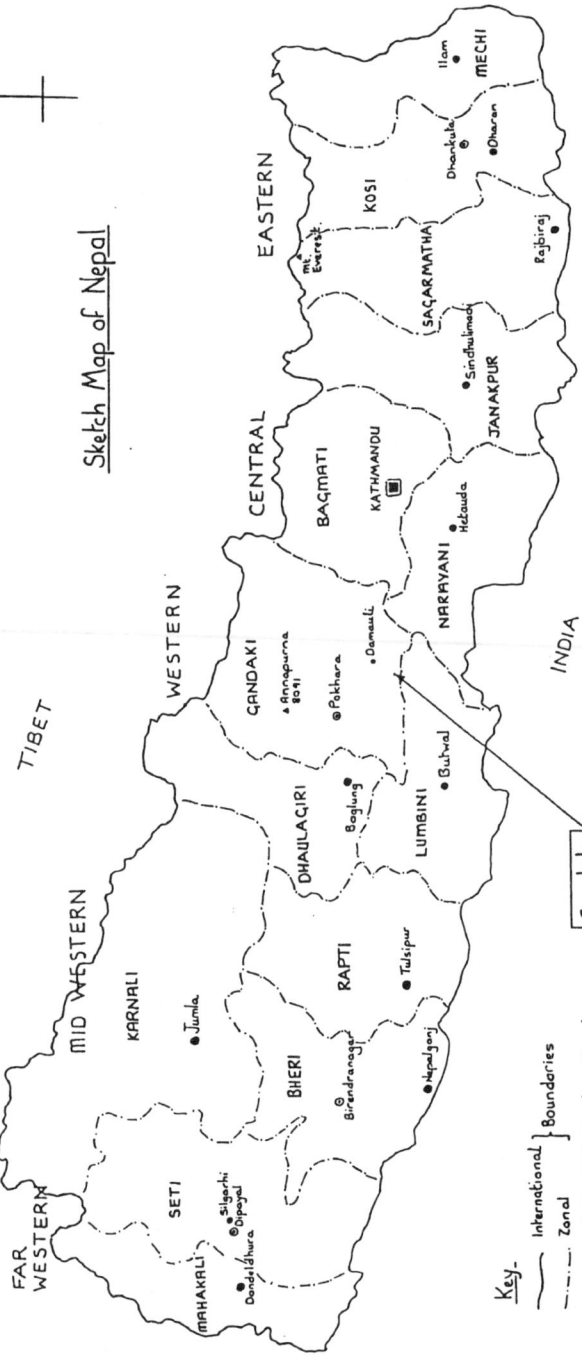

Sketch Map of Nepal

Sketch Map Not To Scale

Key:-
- International ⎫ Boundaries
- ---- Zonal ⎭
■ Capital ◉ Regional ● Zonal

Gumlek

CHINA

TIBET

INDIA

FAR WESTERN

MID WESTERN

WESTERN

CENTRAL

EASTERN

MAHAKALI

SETI

KARNALI

BHERI

RAPTI

DHAULAGIRI

GANDAKI

LUMBINI

NARAYANI

BAGMATI

JANAKPUR

SAGARMATHA

KOSI

MECHI

Dandeldhura
Silgarhi
Dipayal
Jumla
Birendranagar
Nepalganj
Tulsipur
Baglung
Annapurna 8091
Pokhara
Butwal
Damauli
Hetauda
KATHMANDU
Sindhulimadi
mt. Everest
Dhankuta
Rajbiraj
Ilam
Dharan

100

PART III - KATHMANDU

Chapter 12 - THE 'BUS FROM HELL'

In our anxiety to be ready for the bus we awoke far too early the next morning. Gam was getting ready to set off for his village with a rich Japanese benefactor who was paying for a new school to be built there. Before they went we took some photographs of Gam, his wife and two daughters who were home on vacation. Normally they boarded at a very up market private school called St Mary's. This certainly showed in the standard of their English but, as in all private schools, they have to work very hard and had brought home mountains of homework for the holiday. Bill had offered to help Gam produce a hotel brochure using our computer and printing facilities back in England so some of the photos were for that purpose. The cost of printing in Nepal is extremely high and this was the least we could do for him in return for his hospitality. Several shots were taken of Gam standing proudly behind the reception desk talking on the telephone and outside the hotel. We could then select the best ones for printing. Gam is a Buddhist so we received a typical Buddhist farewell when we were each presented with a white shawl or scarf. As well as this we were given a Gurkha knife brooch each. Dear Gam, I do hope he makes a success of his hotel, he certainly deserves to and the motto on the door "Come as a guest, leave as a friend" couldn't be more true.

Ramsingh was supposed to be meeting us at the hotel between 9.30 and 10.00 so that we could give him his present and a tip to be shared between him and the other three porters who had come with us to Gumlek. We hung on till 10.15 but then decided we'd better head for the bus stop, so we left the purple waterproof, together with a 'Kentucky Fried Chicken' baseball cap and the tip, with Gam's wife for Ramsingh to collect. The booking agent, who introduced himself as Krishna, brought out chairs for us to sit on while we waited, our bags stacked up, in the sweltering sun.

"You stay in my hotel next time, cheaper than Twin Peaks, only four dollars a night" he cajoled, handing us his card. This I kept to give to my hard-up student son who would love to go to Nepal but wouldn't be able to afford the luxury of Twin Peaks. The bus was obviously running to 'Nepali time' as it was now nearly 11.00 and there was still no sign of it. However, to our delight, who should come striding down the road but Ramsingh. We greeted him with open arms and Dhane ran back to the Hotel for his present. He had brought one of the Dhan Bahadurs with him and we greeted them both like long lost friends. I think Ramsingh was pleased with the waterproof and I'm sure he was delighted with the tip but although all Nepalis love giving and receiving presents it is not the custom in Nepal to show open gratitude. We promised to see them again when we returned to Nepal and to bring them something from England. With that the bus trundled round the corner and we heaved the baggage onto the roof where it was fastened down rather perfunctorily with a couple of frayed pieces of rope. Had I known what sort of a journey lay ahead of us I would have begged the driver to strap the bags on more securely but, more importantly, if I had known what sort of a bus ride we were in for, I would never have got on the bus at all! However, I am a trusting person and I climbed happily aboard. Bill was a little more apprehensive.

"I hope this bus driver knows what he's doing" he mumbled. "I've heard about this road."

"Oh it'll be all right" I said cheerily, waving goodbye and blowing a kiss out of the window to Ramsingh and Dhan Bahadur. "It's cheaper than the plane anyway."

What price human life? This truly was a 'bus ride from hell' if you'll excuse this well-used phrase. The first part of the journey passed uneventfully enough as the road was so full of potholes and stones that the bus couldn't go any faster than about fifteen miles per hour. We passed through pleasant little villages, stopping at Damauli, looking bright and colourful now in the sunshine - very different from when we had set off to Gumlek in the rain. We stopped to let down or pick up passengers at all the small towns on the way and at every one, street sellers rushed up to the windows selling bananas, cucumbers and various things to refresh us on our journey as well as the usual souvenirs which were thrust through the windows at us. Other passengers included a British canoeing party who got off at a bridge just past Damauli to canoe part of the Seti river. After we had been on the road for some three or four hours the potholes became fewer and we came to a metalled piece of road which even had a white line down the middle in places. We started to climb quite steeply towards Kathmandu and the road started to bend sharply. As I said before, I am a very trusting person and always assume that the person in control knows what he is doing. However, my trust was totally misplaced on this occasion. As the condition of the road improved, the speed of the bus increased, the driver recklessly overtaking anything and everything, relying only on a long and loud hoot of his horn to warn oncoming traffic. We passed a driver, standing by his smashed bus, his passengers nowhere in sight, so this method was obviously not foolproof. As the road climbed, hairpin bends were taken without slowing down in the slightest and with mounting panic, I gripped the pole at the side of my seat. I hardly dared look across at Bill or out of the window where the wheels of the bus were mere inches away from a sheer drop down to the valley below. There was not even a semblance of a barrier on the bends to stop us plunging to the bottom.

"D..d' you think our bags are still on the top?" I whispered, lamely.

"You won't need any bags if he carries on like this - we'll all be over the edge!"

Bill was now putting his boots on.

"What does he think he's playing at! Is he trying to kill us all?" he shouted to Dhane in the seat in front.

Boots on, he stood up ready to go and give the driver a piece of his mind. Dhane, too, was clearly agitated.

"This driver crazy, he drive like a madman!"

Now in Nepal, everyone respects the Gurkhas, so when Dhane stood up and shouted some stern words in Nepalese to the driver, he did slow down. The other passengers, who were mostly Nepalese, merely sat, calmly shaking their heads as if this was just another hiccup in their daily lives. Even the owner of the bus who was sitting across the gangway from us didn't seem to value his bus enough to do more than raise an eyebrow. When the bus stopped for the next tea/loo break, I stumbled down the steps of the bus, tears of relief filling my eyes, and followed the other passengers to what appeared to be the loo. Both Bill and Dhane went and spoke to the driver, reminding him that he was responsible for the lives of his passengers. He looked slightly shame-faced but explained that he was only trying to make up time in order to reach Kathmandu before 6.00 pm as after that time he would have to pay to enter the city. By the time I returned from yet another encounter with a Nepalese loo - this time merely a hole in the ground under a rickety corrugated iron shack - the air was a little calmer. Miraculously our luggage was still on the roof and we had no choice but to climb aboard again for the last leg of the journey. Dhane told us later that, on average, two buses a month go over the edge on this road and we vowed that we would use the internal flight in the future, the £40 air fare being a small price to pay for one's life.

We arrived on the outskirts of Kathmandu just inside the 6 o'clock curfew. It had taken us seven hours to do a journey of only about 200 kilometres! The now familiar dust filled the air and the driver donned his mask, an essential if you spend much time driving in this city. Men, women and children worked at the side of the road, breaking up rocks into smaller stones by hand or toiling up the hill carrying huge loads of stones to deposit them on the heap and then rushing down for another load. Whether they were paid by the load I don't know but the women, thin as laths, were sprinting - as much as their saris would allow - down to the bottom of the hill for their next load and this was at the end of a long working day. It was dusk when we finally reached Dhane's house.

Chapter 13 - DOING THE TOURIST BIT

The next four days before our flight back to England were to be spent being tourists. Kathmandu has to be seen to be believed but four days were enough for me. It has all the hallmarks of cities the world over - the contrast between the wealth and the poverty, the dirt of the back streets and the splendour of the temples, the corruption, danger, busyness and noise - but all this to a much greater degree than any other city I have ever been to. The fact that we were accompanied by a Nepalese Gurkha meant that we were pestered and ripped off less than if we had been on our own, as we discovered when we ventured out without Dhane on the third day.

Our first tourist trip took us to the Thamel area which is in the north west of the city and contains many of the hotels, guest houses and trekking agencies. Consequently it is the main tourist trap for foreigners and the streets are lined with shops selling cheap and colourful clothes, carpets, jewellery and all the crafts we had seen in the Tibetan village - singing bowls, prayer wheels, prayer beads, masks, jewellery, incense burners, statues of Buddha - but in much greater abundance and variety. You could also buy a Berghaus or a Jack Wolfskin rucksack but, selling at a fraction of the cost of the real thing, these were all copies. Bargaining was a must, and all part of the fun. Some stall-holders would come down in price by as much as two thirds, although this varied tremendously from stall to stall. The shops seemed able to charge more than the outside stalls, and needed to, to cover their greater overheads. The street sellers who didn't have a stall or pitch but carried their wares round in a bag slung over their shoulder could offer the best price of all and were also the most persistent, having the advantage of being able to follow us down the street until, hopefully, we gave in and bought something just to get rid of them.

"Come see my stall, I give you good price."

"Come look, see, only looking not buying."

"You buy nice necklace for madam?"

"Looking only cost nothing." These and other persuasive enticements were shouted at us from all quarters and as soon as we ventured within the imaginary demarcation line, stools would be produced for us to sit on and wares would be spread out before us. We could never get away with buying just one thing because there was always a better deal to be had if we bought in bulk. Really, we could have bought all our gifts for friends at home from one or two stalls and made quite a saving as they all sold more or less the same thing, but at this stage it was all new to us. After two or three days we were much more blasé.

As we were with Dhane we were privileged to be his guests for lunch at the Kathmandu Gurkha transit camp and we enjoyed a delicious meal of samosas followed by chicken and noodles, which made quite a change from the rice, *dal* and boiled potatoes we had been eating on the trek. For those without Gurkha connections there are plenty of tourist standard restaurants in Kathmandu with meals at reasonable prices and there is also one Wimpey cafe - a haven in the city - with immaculately clean tables and proper loos with wash basins and toilet paper!

In the afternoon we went to the zoo, hoping for an elephant ride. The elephant, however, was ill so we were disappointed. I do not like zoos at the best of times and this one was one of the poorest kind, with the animals pacing up and down in small cages and the grounds rather neglected. Security, I was relieved to find, was of a better standard than I had been led to expect and the cages and enclosures, if rather tatty and run down, looked reasonably strong. This zoo, like all other zoos in whatever country you go to, seems to be a meeting place for courting couples, although the sort of 'courting' you are likely to see in Britain was strictly taboo and I only ever saw couples shyly holding hands.

A party of very young school children stood, with their hands holding their ears, in a long crocodile by the exit. This was obviously a variation on the 'fingers on lips' or 'hands on heads' ploys used with young children in Britain in the 1950s to keep them quiet. They filed out of the zoo and piled into an ancient van whose capacity seemed to have no limits as more and more little faces pressed up against the back window. We picked up Sandeep and Smriti from school and then called in on Sunita's parents on the way home. While we had been on the Annapurna Base Camp trek, Sunita's younger brother had borrowed Dhane's motorbike and had had an accident, doing quite a bit of damage both to the bike and to himself. As he had not been insured to drive this motorbike and was not in a position to pay for the repairs Dhane was none too happy with him and he, easily identifiable as his face was nearly covered by a huge bandage, was keeping out of Dhane's way.

It seemed that it was only the children who were brave enough to come and practice their English on us. The rest of the family stayed in the background and peeped at us from a distance - another example of education bringing confidence. Back at Dhane's house Smriti showed us some of her school books. The emphasis seemed to be very much on English grammar rather than spoken English. Long lists of verbs had to be declined and such things as strong, stronger, strongest, strange, stranger and strangest were tediously written out. The language in the textbooks was old-fashioned to say the least and the approach to teaching very Victorian. Smiriti read to me from various books of traditional stories such as The Three Bears and The Sleeping Beauty but the language was so archaic that I wondered if she really understood what she was reading. However, when I asked her questions about the story she was able to answer me quite correctly by referring back to the text and forming a very grammatically correct answer, something British children seem to have great difficulty in doing. The lack of opportunity to talk to English speaking people meant that she found conversation more difficult.

That evening Dhane went to a neighbour's house to celebrate their daughter's first menstruation. One would have thought that this, being essentially a milestone in a woman's life, would be a cause for celebration among the women but no, this was another all male 'do' with not a female in sight. Sunita seemed to spend most evenings cooking the evening meal and then clearing up afterwards, which included sweeping and wiping down the whole of the kitchen, so presumably all the other women were occupied in the same way and were too busy to go to parties.

The next day we were to visit the most famous of all the temples, the Swayambhunath Stupa and monastery. This is the one in all the photos, with the 'all seeing eyes'. Our departure was delayed while we waited for Sunita to finish the washing which, of course, all had to be done by hand as well as various other tasks and then while she changed into her best clothes ready for what was to be a trip into the 'West End' of Kathmandu. No self-respecting Nepali woman would venture into town in anything other than her best clothes, and the women provide a blaze of colour as they stroll elegantly in their saris of every shade. Bill and Dhane strode ahead not giving a thought to Sunita, yards behind. It is impossible to take long strides in a sari and Nepalese women look quite as chic as any French woman as they glide gracefully along in a way that only the wearing of a sari can promote.

The temple was surrounded by the usual tourist stalls selling trinkets of every description. The famous monkeys leapt from building to building, pinching the fruit that had been left as offerings to the gods and, being sacred animals, they are not prevented from doing this. Our fifty rupee donation to the Buddhist temple was far in excess of anyone else's but here surely we could be permitted to be more generous? As non-Hindus we were not allowed into the Hindu temple but all around us various ceremonies were going on with garlands and *tika* being presented and gifts offered to the gods. I became confused as to which were the Hindu and which were the Buddhist temples, but seemingly the two religions are very much intertwined, the main difference being that anyone can become a Buddhist but one has to be born a Hindu.

I was determined to take home an example of the national Nepalese dress as worn by the villagers of Gumlek. So, hoping that I would remember how to put it all on, we headed for the equivalent of 'Oxford Street' in Kathmandu. This is a maze of tiny little narrow streets leading off a very wide avenue called the Durbar Marg which is where the king's palace and many of the important government buildings are. The shops appeared to be grouped according to what they sold, so all the material shops were in one area. Brightly coloured cottons in patterns of every description hung over the streets while serious buyers sat inside the shops being shown the various rolls of cloth by the shop assistants. Our first port of call was to buy the long sleeved top called the *cholo* - quite a difficult task as I was several sizes larger that the average Nepalese woman. I followed Sunita up a narrow wooden staircase to the top of the shop where eventually we found one to fit - only just, as it was still a bit short on the sleeve. However, it had a nice red background with a white pattern which I was assured was typical of the ones worn by Nepalese villagers. Sunita very kindly made me a present of this and I shall treasure it always. We then needed five metres of material for the *guni* or skirt, which is wrapped around and pleated at the front a bit like a sari but without the end part that goes over the shoulder. I chose a dark green with red flowers to match the *cholo*. To finish it off I needed another four metres of a slightly narrower cotton for the *patuka* - the piece that winds round and round the waist. The shopkeeper tried to persuade me to have white but I didn't think this would be a very practical colour for working in the fields and went for a bright green. (This was to stain the rubber seal on my washing machine a permanent green when I washed it at home!) The cost per metre was only forty-five rupees so the whole lot had only cost the equivalent of £6. I then bought a sari for 'best' from a trader further up the street. While the *guni* and *patuka* were in a very serviceable cotton material, the sari was of a much lighter synthetic fabric.

By now Dhane and Bill were getting bored and we were due to visit Smriti and Sandeep's school at 3 o'clock so reluctantly we left this fascinating shopping area. It actually boasts one covered shopping precinct with an escalator and Dhane assured us that most Nepalese only came here to ride on the escalator, the shops being far too expensive for them.

We were a bit late for our appointment at the school and the children were already coming out. Feeling rather scruffy in our T-shirts and rucksacks we waited in the foyer and were formally met by the headmaster's secretary who invited us to have a look at the senior part of the school where there would still be some pupils about. My first impression was of a school which was trying in every way possible to emulate the English Public school. Rules were very strict and there were notices everywhere such as "No parents are allowed beyond this point". We were amused by a notice pinned up in the senior part of the school which read as follows:

> There are 3 kinds of people:
> 1 A sponge - which soaks up everything.
> 2 A funnel - things go in one end and out the other.
> 3 A sieve - which sorts out the good from the bad.

On speaking to some of the older pupils it was obvious that they had taken notice of this as they were extremely courteous and polite and seemed honoured to show us around their school. Classes were very large, as many as forty or fifty, and in very small poorly lit classrooms; the equipment was all very old and well-used. Many of the older pupils were boarders and accommodation was spartan. We moved on to the kindergarten where here again the equipment was very old though serviceable. There was an outdoor play area with metal climbing equipment that had rather too many sharp corners to pass strict British Health and Safety regulations. As if to confirm the lack of safety precautions Sandeep had a bandage round his head covering quite a nasty cut he had received from a sharp corner. The head of the nursery department introduced us to her staff and helpers. Here, there were nice small rooms and furniture and the atmosphere was obviously very friendly and caring. The Nepalese sense of discipline and their serious attitude to education was very apparent, even the teachers wore a uniform of red and white saris.

Feeling more confident after our initial forays into Kathmandu with Dhane, we decided to strike out on our own the next day. Armed with a town map and the name of the district where Dhane lived we headed first for the Hindu temples of the Patan area. Following the signposted "Patan Trail" we found many of the temples very dilapidated. Grass and weeds grew out of every nook and cranny and some were in a serious, if not dangerous, state of repair. Progressing to the main square, however, things improved and the more important temples were better cared for. We then took a taxi, back to the Durbar Marg which we had visited the day before. We first enquired whether it had a meter; this is a wise precaution against a common tourist rip-off. In sharp contrast to all the banks, travel agents and government buildings that lined both side of the Durbar Marg, young boys and men were lying asleep on the pavement or on the side of the road. Women with infants on their backs held out begging bowls to us and thin, bony old men, sometimes with a limb missing, sidled up, pointing to their mouths. At least at this time of the year it would not be too cold for them at night. As we came nearer to the shopping area the people on the streets were more likely to be selling something - heaps of spices spread out on pieces of sacking or fruit and vegetables spilling out into the road.

After a luxurious visit to the loo in the Wimpey and a cheeseburger, chips and cup of coffee we found our way back to the maze of narrow streets where we had been the day before, and the Annapurna Seed Shop, which should have been called the Annapurna Spice Shop as it was full of every variety of spice and herb imaginable. Catering expressly for the European market, recipe leaflets were produced using many of the spices on sale. I bought several packets at a fraction of the cost they would be in England including some saffron which, as all cooks know, is horrendously expensive. It is possible to buy the same spices from street sellers who heap them up in great coloured, aromatic piles on the side of the road but is probably safer to buy in packets. Speaking of which, I had now had a couple of days free of diarrhoea and foolishly thought I was over it. This was not to be as, walking nonchalantly through the area selling cotton materials, it struck again and I had to abandon my quest for dress materials to search for a loo. This is an almost impossible task in Kathmandu unless you happen to be in an area of either restaurants or guest houses. None of the shops in this area had toilets and, panic rising, I asked a street trader.

"I take you nice toilets" he said and set off at a fast pace through the narrow streets, dodging the crowds. After what seemed an age and miles of crowded passages we arrived at the 'shopping precinct'.

"In here nice toilets" he waved his hand proudly. Ignoring the requests at the entrance for "Ten rupees please!" I dashed inside. If these were 'nice toilets' I hate to think what the 'not nice' ones were like. There were a couple of individual cubicles with doors that pushed to but did not lock and the whole floor area was awash with water overflowing from a large tank in the middle which was filled by a continuous flow of water from a pipe. This seemed to be the only means of cleaning or flushing the place and was totally ineffectual - I leave the rest to your imagination. (I did visit one slightly worse 'convenience' in a Nepali cafe in a sort of cupboard only about 3' 6" high and just off the kitchen. There was a nine inch gap all round the bottom of the cubicle so that all the rubbish from the floor could also be swilled down the same hole! Anyone who happened to be in this cubbyhole while the floor was being swilled would have had a nasty experience!)

Bill, meanwhile, in gratitude, had given the street trader 20 rupees for his trouble, but not content with this he was at my elbow a few minutes later trying to sell me, what in actual fact turned out to be, a very nice wooden chess set in a turned wooden case. However, at that particular moment I was in no mood for bargaining. When I had recovered somewhat, we wandered further into the maze of passages and finally found the famous Durbar Square - a huge square surrounded by stalls of every description as well as more temples. Here a couple of Nepalese guides tried to buy our daysacs from us.

"Good rucksack, I buy, I give you good price."

"Good English rucksack, I need for guide. You sell?"

We had to be back at Dhane's by about 4 pm as that evening we were going to Nagarkot, hopefully to see Everest as the sun rose the next morning. We made what we thought were some final purchases from one of the many stalls but realised our mistake when we were then mobbed by street traders. The first one showed us one of the chess sets described earlier. Bill has done quite a lot of wood-turning in his spare time and so was quite interested. The price being asked was one thousand rupees but Bill got him down to four hundred and fifty. No sooner had he stowed the chess set safely away in his rucksack than another seller came rushing up.

"I sell you this one for three fifty. This one sandalwood, you smell!" It was, in fact, identical to the one we had already bought, but who could refuse such a bargain? We bought it as well. During all these negotiations young lads buzzed round us like flies offering this and that trinket, and were still following us as we left the square in search of a taxi. Dhane had warned us that anything over about sixty to eighty rupees would be over-charging so we asked the first one:

"How much to Balkhu Pul?"

"Four hundred rupees" was the reply.

"Too much" we said and shook our heads.

"Have you got a meter?" we asked another one.

"Yes, I have meter. Where you go?"

"Balkhu Pul, how much?"

"Three-fifty rupees" he said "Meter not working."

A likely tale, we thought and moved on again. Eventually we found a taxi whose meter was working and paid eighty rupees, but even this included a twenty five percent surcharge which Dhane assured us later that he shouldn't have added on.

70 Hinko Cave, where the tea house had been destroyed by a landslide.

71 Wet through at our favourite lodge, Sinuwa.

72 Dhane and Ramsingh.

73 Ram in a more serious mood.

74 The shoemaker we photographed just above Hot Springs.

75 Annapurna, Hiunchuli and the Modi Khola gorge.

76 Mountain children on the trek to Base Camp.

77 Street traders in Kathmandu.
78 Durbar Square with its many craft stalls.

79 A typical Kathmandu street scene with a Hindu temple in the background.

80 A novel way of displaying wooden flutes.

Chapter 14 - EVEREST AND GOODBYE

We had missed the local bus to Nagarkot but Dhane had arranged for a taxi to take us all and we set off at about 5 o'clock in a relatively new vehicle. The road rose steeply, soon deteriorating into the usual pot-holed track. Suddenly there was a loud bang and the car jolted to a standstill. We had hit something underneath the car which turned out to be a huge boulder sticking up in the middle of the track. We climbed out, telling the taxi driver we'd walk the rest of the way. We all helped to push him off the road, hoping that no serious damage had been done to what was a very smart car compared to most other taxis. We were booked into the very grand sounding Galaxy Hotel which was right at the top of the hill and so would offer the best view of Everest in the morning. It was now quite dark so we stumbled up the rest of the track and finally found the guest house.

Our room was palatial in size with a huge bathroom but, as we had come to expect, the beds and bedding were rather damp and I wished I had brought my sleeping bag. However, undeterred, we dumped our bags and went up to the dining room which was very atmospheric with candles and music and quite an extensive menu. We spent a relaxing evening with Dhane, Sunita and the children. This was our second to last evening and we made the most if it. Plans were made for visits to England in the future and we promised to try and raise some money to bring Sunita and the children over. As the beer took effect we painted idyllic pictures of our house in North Lincolnshire and the seaside at Cleethorpes and even the swings and slide on the village playing field! We waxed lyrical over the Leisure Centre at Cleethorpes and the school swimming pool where women as well as men can bathe, and the beach down the road where you can see seals basking. This was no comparison with the Himalayas, of course, but the children, especially, became quite excited and we are determined to get them over here somehow. We retired early in order to be up by 5 am the next morning to see the sun rise. Even up here we couldn't escape barking dogs and when the pots and pans started clanging in the kitchen at washing up time I gave up all ideas of sleep. Although we were fully clothed the damp from the mattress and bedclothes was insidious and I dozed on and off all night. It was still dark at 5 o'clock when the alarm bleeped us into action. We were among the first on the balcony but gradually one by one, other hotel guests joined us, yawning and stumbling in the cold morning air.

Day dawned over the distant Himalayas casting a pinkish light over the scattered clouds. With the help of a sketched profile borrowed from the hotel we were able to just pick out which particular blip was Everest. After about twenty minutes the clouds gradually covered the range and we tramped off to another part of the hill to view the nearer Langtang and Ganesh peaks. Here again we were not to escape the little boys with their carrier bags of postcards and posters to sell. A little girl even came up to Bill and gave him a flower and then asked for one rupee!

Breakfast was a sumptuous affair with pots of tea and coffee, boiled eggs, toast and jam. The day gradually grew warmer as the sun climbed higher and we walked down the lumpy bumpy track again to wait for the bus back to Kathmandu. Smriti had developed a tummy bug and was feeling sick and had diarrhoea so the plan to stop at Bhaktapur on the way back was abandoned. I was feeling none to sure about my stomach since the experience of the day before and there was a three hundred rupee tax to pay for each tourist entering Bhaktapur. The town itself is very clean as no cars are allowed in the centre but we felt that in view of the tax we would have to pay, we would rather wait until we could have a full day there. The bus promptly broke down two minutes after we set off which meant that we didn't arrive back at Dhane's until about 12.30.

We had the rest of the day to pack, as check-in time at the airport was 6.00 the next morning. I spent the afternoon recording some tapes for Smriti to help her with her English while Bill went for a wander on his own. He didn't take his camera and was largely ignored by the locals, not being obviously a tourist. He explored a few of the side streets of Kathmandu and found the darker, poorer side where families literally lived on the street, surrounded by their rubbish, their children often covered in sores. I was quite pleased not to have gone with him. One knows only too well from the media that every city has its poor and homeless and that being over generous to individuals does not help the country to solve its own problems.

Dhane, meanwhile had gone to one of his various relations in search of some scales, as the Nepalese are very strict about what leaves the country and our luggage was in serious danger of being over the maximum weight of twenty kilos each. After much juggling about, weighing and re-weighing we managed to put all the heavy stuff into our daysacs and get the weight of the rest down to just below forty kilos. The scales must have been pretty accurate as when we checked in at the airport we had just sixty grams to spare!

Dhane and Sunita had cooked a special Nepali dish with pork for our last meal. Unfortunately I couldn't do justice to it but Bill helped me out and we broke open a bottle of beer. It seemed hardly worth setting the alarm for 5.30 am as the usual pre-flight worries and the vivid pictures of our eventful three weeks which kept flashing through my mind precluded any idea of sleep. The dogs kept up their serenade all night long and I daren't use my earplugs for fear of not hearing the alarm.

The air was filled with a thick fog when we stirred ourselves at about 5.00 am - signs of the Kathmandu winter on the way. We carried the bags down and waited in the damp, dark air until about 5.45. The taxi that Dhane had ordered the day before still hadn't arrived so he set off on his motorbike to get another one. Eventually a van met us halfway down the lane to the main road. Smriti, Sandeep and Sunita followed and presented us with garlands they had made and gifts of fruit and put the *tika* on our foreheads which is the customary Hindu farewell. This was the first time I had seen the children in anything warmer than T-shirts and shorts. The air was quite cold at this early hour and they were bundled up in anoraks and woolly hats, Sandeep sporting the Grimsby Town scarf we had given him on our arrival. Dhane, solicitous to the end, shepherded us through the baggage check and we then returned to the entrance to bid our final goodbyes. We knew we would see Dhane again as he was due to return to his barracks in Camberley in about a month's time and we were sure we would see his family before too long either in England or when we returned to Nepal. We finally parted, leaving them for the anonymity of the airport waiting room, our minds full of promises to keep, ideas to develop, friendships to honour, projects to complete, the most important of all being, of course, the building of the new school in Gumlek.

APPENDIX I

KIT LIST

This was the list Tom Langridge gave us which includes most items you will need. All of this we took with us plus additional items in Appendix II.

1   Kit bag or large holdall (or in our case two smaller holdalls each).
2   Daysac.
3   Padlocks - these are useful both for securing luggage and for padlocking the doors of the rooms in the lodges. However, we found that most lodge rooms were supplied with padlocks and keys.
4   Money belt.
5   Camera and film.
6   Passport and visa.
7   Air tickets.
8   Cash and travellers cheques - Nepalese currency can only be obtained in Nepal.
9   Water bottle and mug.
10 Sleeping bag.
11 Lightweight torch or head torch.
12 Notebook and pen/pencil.
13 Book to read.
14 Personal toiletries.
15 Towel - one large and one small are useful.
16 Handkerchiefs.
17 Sweets and nibbles - I took dried apricots and muesli bars.
18 Walking boots and/or trainers.
19 Spare laces.
20 Socks.
21 Underwear.
22 T-shirts/blouses.
23 Trousers and/or skirt, knee length or longer.
24 Fleece jacket or sweater.
25 Sandals/flip-flops.
26 Sun hat/scarf.

27 Sunglasses.

28 2 spare photographs for trek permit.

Medical

1   Water sterilising tablets or iodine drops.

2   Brolene/Optrex and eye-bath.

3   Lip salve with sun block.

4   Antiseptic cream, liquid and wipes.

5   Wet wipes, for when there is no water to wash hands.

6   Lint or pre-packed sterile dressings.

7   Cotton wool.

8   Plasters.

9   Imodium tablets or equivalent.

10 Bandages.

11 Crepe bandage.

12 Throat tablets.

13 Dioralyte or equivalent in case of de-hydration from severe diarrhoea.

14 Cold remedy.

15 Painkillers.

16 Scissors.

17 Malaria tablets.

18 Any other personal medication.

APPENDIX II

I give you here a few 'tips for lady travellers'. Obviously I read all the usual travel and guide books before we set off but the following are a few tips that might be useful to other first-time visitors to Nepal, in addition to the standard kit and medical lists provided in most guide/travel books.

1   Take old clothes - I managed to ruin a couple of decent light-coloured T-shirts with both red *tika* and thick mud stains. If you have any modern synthetic wickable thermal type shirts these are easier to wash and quicker to dry than cotton.

2   Similarly, your skirt (or baggy trousers for the more touristy areas) is better in a fine, light material.

3   A skirt pocket is useful for things like lip salve, loo paper and also a polythene bag in which to put used loo paper after urinating. Obviously toilet paper used for anything more serious should be burned or buried.

4   Tampax and pads should be carried whether or not your period is due, with plenty of polythene bags to collect up used ones until a suitable place can be found to dispose of or burn them. Don't think that just because your period is not due that you will be OK, as strenuous trekking can totally disrupt the menstrual cycle. I had carefully organised the taking of my contraceptive pill so as to ensure that I would not have a period while in Nepal, but to no avail. A few days walking brought everything forward and the only thing available at the tea-houses is a rather coarse bright pink toilet paper. Pads can be bought in the towns but are expensive and tampons are almost impossible to find anywhere.

5   Salt for the leeches. If you smoke, a lighted cigarette gets them off but if you don't smoke, the flame from a cigarette lighter or match can tend to burn more than just the leech!

6   Even if you are doing fairly low-level trekking where the night time temperatures are fairly warm, a sleeping bag is useful to lie on, with a sheet over the top of you, as mattresses in the lodges tend to be damp.

7 A waterproof bag for the sleeping bag is useful in case your porters aren't as efficient as ours were in making sure their packs were protected with polythene in the rain.

8 Some sort of energy giving powder to add to your water - both to disguise the taste of the iodine or chlorine purifier and to give you much needed energy.

9 Cup-a-soup for when you don't feel like eating much, for example, at altitude, or for a warming snack.

10 Sweets to hand out to children on the way. These are small enough gifts to be acceptable rather than encouraging begging.

11 A small, collapsible plastic bowl for washing hands, hankies, underwear so that you can tip the water away afterwards on the ground and not pollute the streams.

12 Plenty of wet wipes and antiseptic wipes for when you can't find any water to wash your hands.

13 Things with a dual purpose like spare boot laces which can be tied together to make a washing line, or spare socks that double as mitts.

14 Any items of clothing or footwear, especially warm clothing, that can be fitted into to your luggage weight allowance - useful to give to porters.

15 If you are hiring porters yourself it is better to fix a slightly higher daily rate exclusive of meals so that they have to budget for their own meals. This may sound mean but you will be amazed how much porters will eat, especially if it is at your expense!

16 Buy packets of dried noodles for the porters which can be re-constituted with hot water. This will save the porters money on food as you get higher up and meals become more expensive.

17 Take cotton hankies rather than loads of tissues. They are easy to wash out under a tap or in water from a stream and do not pose a disposal problem. They also have other uses, and can be dipped in stream to cool you off or used as emergency first aid for minor injuries.

18 An umbrella is useful both for the rain and as a sunshade.

Finally, do take little treats for yourself for when you tire of rice and *dal*, but not chocolate which tends to melt in the heat. You could also take small amounts of things to pamper yourself like a nice body lotion, face or hand cream.

Appendix III

GLOSSARY OF NEPALESE WORDS

ama	-	mother
biraami	-	sick, ill
bistaare	-	slowly
brahmin	-	high caste Hindu - the only caste allowed to be priests
chakati	-	sitting mat
cholo	-	Nepalese blouse worn by the women
dal	-	traditional Nepalese thick soup made with lentils, soy beans or chick peas and flavoured with spices
danyabad	-	thank you
dhoti	-	knee length piece of cloth wrapped around the waist, worn by the men for working in
doko	-	large basket carried on the back with a strap to go round the head, for carrying heavy loads
guni	-	long length of material worn like a skirt by the women, similar to a sari
hacia	-	curved reaping knife
kachhad	-	longer version of the **dhoti**
kainjadi	-	flat, single skinned drum
khola	-	river
madal	-	long, cylindrical, double-skinned drum
malai phul ramro	-	I like flowers
mero naam Anne ho	-	my name is Anne
mit	-	adopted brother/relation
mitini	-	wife of above
mo-mo	-	finely ground meat made into meatballs inside a suet pastry-like parcel, either steamed or fried

namaste	-	Nepalese greeting at any time of the day
oraalo	-	downhill
pani parena	-	it has stopped raining
pani paryo	-	it's raining
patuka	-	long piece of material wound round the waist as a belt and back support
phul	-	flower
pul	-	bridge
raksi	-	colourless Nepalese spirit distilled from millet or soy beans
shyakhu	-	umbrella
theki	-	wooden or clay pot used for butter or yoghurt
tika	-	red mark made with red powder and/or rice, put on forehead as a welcome or in ceremonies
ukaalo	-	uphill

APPENDIX IV

READING LIST

Below are some suggestions for further reading.

1. Lonely Planet guide - Nepal. Publisher, Lonely Planet Publications.
2. Trekking in Nepal. A Traveller's Guide. By Stephen Bezruchka. Publisher, Cordee.
3. Trekking in the Annapurna Region. By Bryn Thomas. Publisher, Trailblazer Publications.
4. Nelles Guide - Nepal. By Robertson McCarta and Nelles Verlag.
5. Culture Shock, Nepal. By Jon Burbank. Publisher, Kuperard.
6. Annapurna, A Trekker's Guide. By Kev Reynold. Publisher, Cicerone Press.
7. Trekking in the Everest Region. By Jamie McGuinness. Publisher, Trailblazer Publications.
8. Footloose in the Himalayas. By Mike Harding. Publisher, Mermaid Books, Penguin Group.
9. Nepali for Trekkers - Phrase book and tape. By Stephen Bezruchka. Publisher, The Mountaineers.
10. Lonely Planet Nepali Phrasebook. By Mary-Jo O'Rourke with Bimal Shrestha. Publisher, Lonely Planet Publications.
11. Nepali - English, English-Nepali Dictionary. By Prakash A. Raj. Publisher, Hippocrene Books, New York.
12. Get By in Nepalese. By Harka Gurung. Publisher, Ratna Pustak Bhandar.
13. Basic Course in Spoken Nepali. By Tika B.Karki and Chij K. Shrestha.

The last two books we bought in Kathmandu so they may not be available in the UK.